SPIRITUALLY
INCORRECT

SPIRITUALLY INCORRECT

FINDING GOD IN ALL THE WRONG PLACES

DAN WAKEFIELD

ILLUSTRATIONS BY MARIAN DELVECCHIO

Walking Together, Finding the Way
SKYLIGHT PATHS® Publishing
Woodstock, Vermont

Spiritually Incorrect:
Finding God in All the Wrong *Places*

2004 First Printing
Text © 2004 by Dan Wakefield
Illustrations © 2004 by Marian DelVecchio

Library of Congress Cataloging-in-Publication Data
Wakefield, Dan.
Spiritually incorrect : finding God in all the wrong places / Dan Wakefield ; illustrations by Marian DelVecchio.
    p. cm.
ISBN 1-893361-88-8
1. Spiritual life—Christianity. I. DelVecchio, Marian. II. Title.
BV4501.3 .W34 2003
248.4—dc21

                                                                                        2003014025

Manufactured in United States of America
10   9   8   7   6   5   4   3   2   1

SkyLight Paths Publishing is creating a place where people of different spiritual traditions come together for challenge and inspiration, a place where we can help each other understand the mystery that lies at the heart of our existence.

SkyLight Paths sees both believers and seekers as a community that increasingly transcends traditional boundaries of religion and denomination—people wanting to learn from each other, walking together, finding the way.

SkyLight Paths, "Walking Together, Finding the Way" and colophon are trademarks of LongHill Partners, Inc., registered in the U.S. Patent and Trademark Office.

Walking Together, Finding the Way
Published by SkyLight Paths Publishing
A Division of LongHill Partners, Inc.
Sunset Farm Offices, Route 4, P.O. Box 237
Woodstock, VT 05091
Tel (802) 457-4000 Fax (802) 457-4004
www.skylightpaths.com

To my "family" in Miami:
Virginia, Manuel, and Karina Perez
Karina and Kalel Corrales

Be kind; for everyone you meet is
fighting a great battle.

—Philo of Alexandria

We must take God as he comes to
each of us.

— Father Nicholas Morcone,
Glastonbury Abbey

CONTENTS

ACKNOWLEDGMENTS

Much of the material herein originally appeared in my column "Spiritually Incorrect" on the Internet website Beliefnet.com. For the opportunity to write the column I thank my editor Anne Simpkinson and publisher Steve Waldman. Other material has appeared in the *New York Times Magazine*, *The Nation*, *Common Boundary*, *The Sun*, *Christian Century*, and *Yoga Journal*.

I

A Guide to Spiritual Incorrectness

committed my first violation of political correctness when the term came into national prominence in the early 1990s. Reviewing a novel for a prominent Sunday book review, I referred to a character the way the author had described him, as the heroine's "crippled lover." An editor huffily told me that "We don't use *that word*" (crippled), and proceeded to instruct me to describe the character by the actual nature of his affliction. I dutifully changed it to "her club-footed lover," which seemed harsher to my own ear, but the editor approved. I made matters worse by asking if this change were part of being "politically correct," not realizing that it was politically incorrect to acknowledge that there was such a thing as political correctness, much less suggest that it was used in making an editorial judgment. I haven't been asked to review there again.

At that time I hadn't yet learned that Smith College, always on the cutting cultural edge, had issued to its incoming students in 1990, the dawning of the age of political correctness, a *Guide* to politically correct language. This official document suggested that people formerly referred to as "disabled" or "handicapped" should now be called "differently abled," in order to "underline the concept that differently abled individuals … are not less or inferior in any way." In a list of "Specific

Manifestations of Oppression," the Smith *Guide* defined "ableism" as "oppression of the differently abled, by the temporarily able."

To check on his views of the new terminology I called my friend Leonard Kriegel, who has had to negotiate life on crutches or in a wheelchair since he was stricken by polio at age eleven. Kriegel writes with passion and eloquence about why he is proud to be called "a cripple," and assured me he had no plans to replace that term with a newer model.

"'Differently abled' doesn't mean a damn thing," he said. "There's a fundamental difference between having braces on your teeth and braces on your legs, and it's nonsense to pretend otherwise."

Further challenging orthodoxies when I asked him about his religious views, Kriegel told me, "I wouldn't call myself a believer but a man yearning for belief—which is also why I wouldn't call myself a nonbeliever." Wow. Kriegel was not only "politically incorrect," he was even "atheistically incorrect."

I first sniffed the scent of "*spiritual* correctness" when the subject of diet and exercise was raised at a conference on Conscious Aging. One of the leaders allowed that such practices were acceptable *if* done for reasons of health, rather than to try to make yourself look better. Beware! Striving to improve one's appearance was an ego trap (or trip), a subject of scorn.

The audience responded warmly to this teaching, consigning those superficial folks who cared about their looks to an outer circle beyond the pale of the spirit, a Dante-esque hell of continuous preening and moaning over their mirrors, reflecting only emptiness. The speaker poked fun at those models of aging who tried to stay young, like older men climbing mountains, and "sisters doing yoga at one hundred!" The audience laughed along.

I winced, realizing I was now in violation of a new code of correctness, for these mountain climbing old guys and "sisters doing yoga" are the elders I admire, those I try to emulate. I take yoga and tai chi classes, and go every year to health spa Rancho La Puerta in Mexico to rise at dawn for the mountain hikes. And I have to confess that I don't just want to be healthy, I want to feel—and yes, even *look* better!

Believing there must be other stifled souls who would like to indulge in such behavior—and breathe the fresher, freer air of spiritual incorrectness—I am sharing my own confessions, thoughts, and ideas. In the spirit of the Sanksrit word "namaste," I honor the light within you. May we all find God—by whatever name—however and wherever She comes to each of us.

1

Does God Care If You Drive a Convertible?

My blatant violation of the code of spiritual correctness came at age sixty-five, when, annoyed by what I thought of as my "turkey neck" of flabby flesh, I signed up for cosmetic surgery and got a face-lift. I later read in an article in *Christianity Today* that, at least in one contemporary Christian view, such doctoring of the flesh isn't approved. The article by a "Christian physician" noted that there are "abuses" in all branches of medicine, and while cosmetic surgery is valid for treating serious burns, "It is the same technique used for tummy tucks and face-lifts." Such practices were obviously seen as frivolous, if not un-Christian.

A year after I elected to have the cosmetic surgery I underwent a nonelective surgery—meaning I had to have it if I elected to live any longer—a triple-bypass heart operation. After surviving that one, I was even less concerned about other people's judgments and opinions, so I brazenly ventured even farther out into the wilds of spiritual incorrectness. I got my first convertible—a sporty little Mitsubishi Eclipse Spyder. I am not a "car person," and don't even know a BMW from a Saab on sight, so the idea was not to upgrade my motoring status, but to feel the fun and freedom of driving with the top down, the sun and sea breezes sweeping over me. As far as I'm concerned, a beat-up Chevy convertible that still runs after several hundred thousand miles would do the job as well. This is about feeling the wind and sun, not about striving for some kind of automotive social status.

Some critics of the spiritually correct school see this not as a result of my wanting to enjoy the beautiful scenery where I live by the sea, but falling under the dire influence of a decadent city. Miami Beach might well be the capital of spiritual *in*correctness. On learning I lived in such a Sodom and Gomorrah, a woman I met at a yoga retreat warned me that if I didn't watch out I'd soon be driving a convertible. I admitted I already did, and, even more shocking, it was red. She got up to refill her miso and never returned.

Now I was on a roll. If it is spiritually incorrect to try to improve your physical appearance, it is even less acceptable to decorate your body, and it's a special taboo for a man to adorn himself with jewelry. When a Cuban woman friend gave me a gold chain and bracelet I told her such things were not worn in the WASP Midwest where I grew up, or literary New York, or staid Boston where I'd lived before moving to the torrid zone of Miami.

"I've never worn anything like this," I said to my friend. "Well," she said smiling, "it's about time."

Why not? I thought.

The gold chain and matching bracelet go with the red convertible and the face-lift. A year or so later I violated another rule of spiritual—as well as social—correctness, and got my first tattoo. Even more shocking, it was my own idea! The tattoo is not in a place on my body seen by the public, but, on my honor as a former Eagle Scout, I assure you it is there.

Regardless of how incorrect it may be to have a tattoo, a gold necklace, and a red convertible, none of that has interfered with my prayers or meditation or yoga practice, or the way I try to teach my workshops in Spiritual Autobiography, or my desire to write as truly as possible about subjects I regard as sacred, from sexual to spiritual (and the effort to convey that such subjects are not really separate or isolated from the rest of life).

Sitting on my new tattoo, with face lifted, and gold chain and bracelet dangling, I drive to the beach with the top down in my red convertible, thinking of my favorite prayer from Ted Loder's *Guerrillas of Grace: Prayers for the Battle.* I ask "to grow new each day / To this wild amazing life / You call me to live…"

I had to come up with a definition of *spirituality* when I wrote a book called *The Story of Your Life: Writing a Spiritual Autobiography.* I had never written any kind of how-to book before, and I realized I didn't know how to do it. I figured that the first essential was to define "it," in this case "it" being spirituality, and after rereading some of the great spiritual thinkers for clues and finding little that was helpful as well as concise, out of frustration I turned to my *Oxford English Dictionary* and looked up the word *spirit:*

> *The animating or vital principle in humans (and animals); that which gives life to the physical organism, in contrast to its purely material elements; the breath of life.*

This is my favorite definition of the term, for it doesn't put any religious limitations on the idea of spirituality; rather, it suggests that we all have a spirit. To carry that idea a step further, we all must then be in some basic way *spiritual.* This may seem an insult to some, and a kind of extra dividend to others, who may feel a kind of surprised delight to realize it, like the Bourgeois Gentleman in Molière's play who is thrilled to discover that all his life he's been *speaking prose!*

No doubt some atheists or even agnostics may rebut my definition that includes all humans—even them!—as possessing a spiritual aspect as part of their very humanity. Though my "spiritually incorrect" views and behavior have raised the orthodox hackles of all faiths, especially those of my fellow Christians who are of fundamentalist persuasion, the fact that I write about spirituality at all is most shocking (if not downright offensive) to some of my old atheist/agnostic pals from the literary world. One of my few friends from that world who also writes now about spiritual subjects told me that a mutual friend from the literary ranks said he couldn't read something she had written in that realm, explaining, "It's not my cup of gumbo." That's become our password for our comrades who scorn or are simply left cold by these subjects that fascinate us: It's not their cup of gumbo. That's their taste, and I have no quarrel with it. I'm glad it hasn't really severed any good friendships. My purpose is not to proselytize, either in what I say in conversation or the talks or workshops I give, or in what I write. My aim is rather to bear testimony to my own experience, to convey "this is what happened to me" in matters of the spirit or "this is what I found to be useful in my own search."

When friends who have no interest in such matters ask with genuine curiosity why I write about religion and spirituality, I quote Michael Murphy, the founder of the Esalen Institute, who told me once that "the great game, the game of games, the story of stories is the unfolding of the Divine." But that still begs the question of how a nice, Columbia graduate, Greenwich Village writer, author of books like *Going All the Way* (described by Kurt Vonnegut as "the truest and funniest sex novel any American will ever write"), returned in middle age to the faith of his childhood, and wrote books that had *God* or *Spiritual* in the title (*How Do We Know When It's God?* and *Returning: A Spiritual Journey*)?

That's a legitimate question, a question I answer in telling about …

2

My Spiritually Incorrect
Journey Back to God

When I passed my forty-fifth birthday with no more than the usual ups and downs of a middle-aged writer, I figured I had beat the much-publicized midlife crisis that supposedly bedeviled men of my age. I even began to take pride in my seemingly safe passage through the rocky years that are said to shake up so many middle-aged males (our gender's counterpart of menopause). I went so far as to satirize the whole notion of a midlife crisis in reviewing a book about it.

What midlife crisis? I wanted to know. What's the big deal about hitting your mid- to late forties?

I was unfazed by such stuff, and arrogant in my evident immunity. Wasn't I a hotshot novelist summoned to Hollywood to write my own prime-time television series on NBC *(James at 15)*? The only crisis I foresaw was in the Nielsen ratings.

Three years later my life fell apart. I quit the TV series in a squabble with the censors (they wouldn't allow any reference to birth control when our teenage hero makes love for the first time). The series wasn't renewed for a second season, and after getting one TV movie on the air and having three rejected, I was no longer hot. I found myself swallowed up in the machinery of Hollywood, slogging to one meeting after another, making my sales pitch (a degrading ritual that Sally Struthers called "tap dancing") for ideas that were turned down with numbing regularity. Joan Didion, who knew me since our early days in New York in the fifties, said, "Wakefield, I'll bet you're a lousy meeting." She was right. In Hollywood terms, that was as degrading as being judged a lousy lay. I felt like a West Coast update of Willy Loman.

In the course of the last six months of this downward spiral, I left the work I was doing, the place where I was living, the woman I had lived with for seven years and had thought (hoped) was my mate for life. I went to the doctor with a pounding heart and was told my resting pulse was 120—a condition called tachycardia. After taking an EKG and finding nothing wrong with my heart, the doctor said, "Tell me. Are you in the entertainment business?"

He diagnosed my condition as stress and prescribed beta blockers. When I got home from the doctor's office I called American Airlines and booked the next flight to Boston. I fled to my former adopted hometown that April of 1980, broke and feeling broken. My father died in May and my mother in November. I felt hollowed out inside.

God or fortune or fate led me to Dr. Howard Hartley, then head of the Stress Clinic at Massachusetts General Hospital, who got me on a diet and exercise program for the first time in my life. Following doctor's orders kept me alive and sane, cutting my racing pulse in half and taking off twenty pounds of fat. Dr. Hartley and nurse Jane Sherwood seemed like guardian angels who had stepped out of *It's a*

Wonderful Life to catch me at the edge of a cliff and gently guide me back to solid ground.

When they asked me to go for a month without a drink, I gulped and achieved what seemed the impossible. I'd been stocking in a case of wine in half-gallons every week for the last few years of Hollywood and guzzling it every night, like essential fuel, continuing the habit in Boston. In that month of my longest dry spell since college, a previously unthinkable desire bubbled up, and it wasn't for Chardonnay.

As a child in Indianapolis I was deeply moved by a Baptist Bible school I attended with friends from my grade school. I felt a deep connection with Jesus and a tangible if innocent faith, leading me to decide on my own to be baptized by full immersion when I was eleven years old. As a Boy Scout, that faith was deepened in nature, on overnight hikes and at camp. By the end of high school, though, my all-out adolescent angst and rebellion turned me from faith to cynicism, a switch that was completed and solidified when I went to college at Columbia. I graduated as a full-fledged intellectual atheist. If atheists had membership cards, I'd have carried one.

I substituted Hemingway's "Our nada who art in nada" (from his story "A Clean, Well-Lighted Place") for the Lord's Prayer, and alcohol became my daily Communion. It was not until the horror of a hungover morning at the end of the darkening Hollywood days—just before my forty-eighth birthday—that I reached in desperation for a long-forgotten Bible on my bookshelf and read the Twenty-Third Psalm aloud, finding in its cadence a comfort as welcome as water in a parched land.

I recited the psalm in my head when I sat on my favorite bench in the Boston Public Garden, a special resonance coming with the line "He leadeth me beside the still waters." But it wasn't until the month I stopped drinking—my body and mind cleared of booze for the first time in a quarter-century—that an impulse arose to take the next step. I was sitting in a neighborhood bar on Beacon Hill (though I wasn't drinking I still went to bars out of habit and to hang out with friends) when a housepainter named Tony remarked that he was going to mass on Christmas Eve, just a week away. As if a lightbulb had come on in my head, I thought, "I want to do that too."

I didn't even know what church to go to—any Protestant church would do—and I resorted to searching the *Boston Globe* religion page. King's Chapel was not only close, but its Christmas Eve program seemed nonthreatening: "Candlelight service with carols." Little did I know the minister would add some readings between carols, one of them from an Evelyn Waugh novel called *Helena,* about the mother of Constantine. It spoke of the "latecomers" to the manger—like the latecomers to church—and I guiltily thought I'd been fingered, and the message was addressed to me personally. Still, I screwed up my courage to return for Easter, and then, what was even more challenging, I began to go to church on what I thought of as "regular Sundays." Any normal citizen can go to church at Christmas and Easter without raising an atheist's eyebrow, but I still regarded someone who just goes to church on a regular basis as a bit of a zealot. When I walked through the Boston Common on Sunday mornings that first year, I pulled my coat collar up and kept my head down, hoping none of my intellectual-literary friends would spot me.

I found myself drawn not only to Sunday services, but also to classes taught by our low-key, high-awareness minister, the Reverend Carl Scovel, who seemed to give sermons and lessons designed especially for my needs and questions. He even passed on just the right books at the right time—like *Reaching Out,* by the Catholic theologian Henri Nouwen, and *A Palpable God,* by the prize-winning novelist and eloquent Christian writer Reynolds Price. (I later went to Durham, North Carolina, where Price teaches at Duke, to meet and interview him for a magazine piece, as I began to combine my writing with my spiritual search.)

Having shut out anything religious for most of my adult life, I now felt an almost physical thirst for understanding, information, and guidance. I wrote a note to our minister that I now looked forward to coming to his classes on the New Testament with the eagerness I once felt at the prospect of a free martini party! I went out one cold rainy night to the Parish House for a Bible study class led by Sue Spencer, a former lawyer who was serving as our seminarian while she studied at Harvard Divinity School. At first I was disappointed that only two other people showed up, but as we delved into the story of Jesus healing blind Bartimeus I began to feel the specialness of the gathering, the warmth and the light of the Parish House, and the comradeship of these fellow seekers. I knew for the first time the meaning of Jesus' saying that "Where two or three are gathered together in my name, there I am also." How contrary this was to the lust for the largest audience of those who worship the

Nielsen ratings (as I had so recently in what now seemed a long-ago life).

Along the way I even learned what denomination I was in when I joined King's Chapel, a detail I hadn't even noticed when I started going back to church. We were one of the few Christian congregations within the Unitarian-Universalist Association, which is mostly Humanist, making us an anomaly, jestingly referred to by others in the denomination as the "St. Peter's of the Unitarians." Our Sunday bulletin described the church as "Congregational in governance, Unitarian in theology, and Anglican in worship" (we used our version of the *Book of Common Prayer,* and offered Communion once a month). When I tried to explain all this to outsiders, I pointed out that King's Chapel, which is on the Freedom Trail, is more than three hundred years old, and you could just think of it as "a Boston church."

The theological stew of King's Chapel suited me fine, since the Christianity matched my roots, and the openness of the Unitarians suited my nondogmatic approach to religion. I have learned and benefited from many different spiritual paths, from the Judaism that's the whole basis of Christianity (see *To Life!* by Rabbi Harold Kushner), to the teachings of Zen and the other Eastern religions whose physical/meditative practices have enriched my own faith.

I never felt I was "born again," which suggests some booming voice coming to you out of the blue or lightning striking your forehead. I was relieved when Reverend Scovel told me the word for "conversion" in both Hebrew and Greek was a word that meant "turning," which seemed to fit my own experience. I learned that each turn, no matter how small, changes the course of your path, until you look around one day and realize you are going in a whole different direction than you were a few years ago!

I also learned that one spiritual experience leads to the next. I used to ridicule people who said one drug leads to the next, that beer probably leads to bourbon, marijuana may lead to cocaine or heroin, but I realized it was true, at least in my own experience and that of so many friends. It was also true in the spiritual realm, where going to church could lead to Bible study and retreats, exercise and diet may lead to tai chi and yoga, and all those disciplines that awaken the body and mind and spirit lead you away from the abuse of alcohol and drugs that numb your senses.

I have not become, nor do I aspire to be, a guru or saint or minister. Whatever "ministry" I have, in the broadest sense, is my writing about my own spiritual journey, and giving workshops in Spiritual Autobiography and Releasing the Creative Spirit at churches, synagogues, adult education centers, and prisons across the country. I am nourished and enlivened by this opportunity to give back something to others, a reward that reminds me of these words of Albert Schweitzer to a graduating class of medical students: "I don't know what your destiny will be, but one thing I know. The only ones among you who will be really happy are those who have sought and found how to serve."

What I've given in books and workshops I learned in the courses I took from my minister, Carl Scovel, and all I've absorbed from truly wise men and women of different faiths like the rabbis Harold Kushner and Nancy Flam, and the Roman Catholic priests Henri Nouwen and Father Nicholas

Morcone, the abbot of Glastonbury Abbey, a Benedictine monastery outside Boston that's become a touchstone of my own faith. I've been guided in spirit as well as in the body by the tai chi teacher David Zucker and yoga teachers like Carol Nelson in Boston; Beryl Bender Birch in New York; and Phyllis Pilgrim, Jenni Fox, Paul Gould, and Michelle Hebert at Rancho La Puerta. I have deepened my faith through programs of personal growth like the Forum, given by Landmark Education, and physical recharging at the health spa Rancho La Puerta in Mexico.

In the twenty years since I returned to faith, I have learned the truth William James reports in *Varieties of Religious Experience:* "Nothing is more common in the pages of religious biography than the way in which seasons of lively and of difficult faith are described as alternating." I have known the whole range now, from anger and disillusionment, to honeymoon to separation. Yet the "separation" was never from losing faith in God, but from losing faith in my ability to be in contact, in tune, in harmony, in communication (I don't mean hearing voices but sensing a closeness or rapport) with the Holy Spirit.

In my darkest time, when my efforts to follow a spiritual path had led me to a marriage I knew was impossible the moment we walked out of the church, I found I could no longer pray with words. I had said "I do" when I couldn't, in a sacred ceremony, and now all words mocked me; the prayers and psalms and hymns that had refreshed and comforted me now seemed hollow. Silence became my solace. I turned again to yoga, and the silent movements of the body became my prayer, the only one that seemed genuine then.

Eventually, the words came back, but the silence kept me going, the spirit working through the body rather than the mind. In trying to answer the question "How do we know when it's God?" I have come to trust the body over the mind; while conflicting messages rage in the head, the calmness or the agitation of the body has become my best guide.

There was a calmness and sense of "rightness," of being "on the path" (what the Navajos call "on the gleaming way") when a series of unexpected events led me in 1994 to move to the last place in the world I ever thought I would live—Miami Beach. I smiled as I remembered the lines from the Book of John: "The wind bloweth where it listeth, and thou hearest the sound thereof, but canst not tell whence it cometh, and whither it goest: so is everyone that is born of the spirit." If that's a test of being "born of the spirit," I pass with flying colors.

I have not joined a church here, and in my heart I will always think of King's Chapel in Boston as my church. I now attend with gratitude and pleasure the Coral Gables Congregational Church, where Reverend Donna Schaper provides an inspiring ministry of social justice and courage as well as spiritual depth and meaning. I met Reverend Schaper through our mutual publisher, SkyLight Paths, and have given a workshop and talks at her church, but I didn't start going to Sunday services there until I started taking my goddaughter to its art programs for children and its Sunday School. In more ways than this, my goddaughter, Karina Corrales (age seven at the time of this writing), has become a blessing of the Spirit in my life.

I agree with author Reynolds Price, who has taught for thirty years at Duke University, that "teaching is very much a form of religious work, though I certainly don't set out specifically or secretly to proselytize my students in any direction." I feel the same way about my own teaching, not only in my workshops in Spiritual Autobiography and Creativity, but also in the writing classes I teach as writer-in-residence at Florida International University.

I see the spiritual side of teaching in what Rabbi Nancy Flam, cofounder of the Jewish Healing Center in San Francisco, calls "the ministry of presence." Rabbi Flam told me that, in her service of healing, "I never try to give any advice, I just try to be fully present to the person." Being fully present to another person (rather than thinking about what we're having for dinner or what we should have done yesterday) is one of the great services we can do for them. I try to bring that kind of presence to my students.

Through all the ups and downs, the unexpected turns and challenges of trying to follow a spiritual path, of trying to find "the way," I have sometimes lost faith in my ability to find God or know Her or His will, but never in the reality of God's presence. My own experience was most eloquently summed up by a student at one of my workshops. I was leading a class in Spiritual Autobiography at a conference sponsored by *Image: A Journal of Religion and the Arts* when Wendy M. Wright, a professor of theology at Creighton University in Omaha, read aloud these words she had just composed in a brief writing exercise:

How dark the seeing. How fragmentary. Mostly it consists of learning to free fall. Learning to trust the constant somersaulting. Learning to live with spiritual vertigo.

Learning to love the darkness. Learning to trust the brief glimpses. Learning that blindness is its own seeing. Learning that the falling is in itself beautiful. That at the bottom of the well of my heart, I free fall into You.

To which I add my own "Amen."

II

The Spiritually
Incorrect Outlook

I went to college at Columbia to study with Mark Van Doren, a Pulitzer Prize–winning poet and legendary professor who influenced generations of students, from the Trappist monk Thomas Merton to the Beat writers Allen Ginsberg and Jack Kerouac. (After taking Van Doren's Shakespeare course, Kerouac quit the Columbia football team to devote more time to writing.) In a course called The Narrative Art, in which we read Homer, the Bible, Dante, Cervantes, and Kafka, Van Doren lectured on the New Testament and shocked me into attention one day when he spoke about Jesus.

"Many of you," he said, "got the idea in Sunday school that Jesus was a kind of wispy figure, floating around Jerusalem in a nightshirt." But this was not the Jesus described in the New Testament, he pointed out. The Jesus of the Gospels, he said, was in fact "the most ruthless of men."

That was the first interesting thing I'd heard about Christianity since I'd given up my childhood faith. It didn't reconvert me, but it gave me a new, interesting image of Jesus that went against the "country club" Christianity of the 1950s, when going to church was being sold as a way to find success in business. It woke me up.

Van Doren's observation not only was spiritually incorrect, but made me realize that Jesus himself was spiritually incorrect—hanging out with prostitutes and lepers, tax collectors and outcasts of all kinds, telling a rich man he had as much of a shot at getting into heaven as a camel going through the eye of a needle. Telling people that in order to save their life they had to lose it. Dying on a cross.

And Buddha was just as bad—leaving the wealth of the kingdom to go sit under a tree! The great spiritual leaders of all the major faiths have been spiritually incorrect, going against the easy assumptions of their time, challenging the status quo, having the audacity to wake people up. Refusing to give them easy answers.

I don't like easy answers for the simple reason that I don't believe there are any. When I came of age in the 1950s, those country club Christians had made religion sound like a kind of get-rich-quick scheme; today's equivalent is the self-help message of the books and workshops suggesting that spirituality will make you not necessarily rich but, even better, *happy.*

The poet John Ciardi used to say sometimes before reading a new verse that he had "committed a poem." In that same spirit I report that twice I have "committed" my own versions of "how to" books and given workshops based on them—*The Story of Your Life: Writing a Spiritual Autobiography* and *Releasing the Creative Spirit: Unleash the Creativity in Your Life.* I have refrained from offering any quick fixes or suggesting that any religious or spiritual beliefs or practices will guarantee wealth, success, or happiness, produce great books, symphonies, or paintings, much less cure cancer, or even the common cold. I believe that what we call miracles do happen, but not by request or petition, and most likely in the way that Willa Cather expressed in *Death Comes for the Archbishop*:

> *Miracles ... seem to me to rest not so much upon faces or voices coming suddenly near to us from afar off, but upon our own perception being made finer, so that for a moment our eyes can see and our ears can hear what is there about us always.*

Being spiritually incorrect does not, in my view, mean blasphemy. I respect all sincerely held religious and spiritual beliefs but do not believe in forcing them on others. I have learned that labels are usually misleading, and what's important are the people behind them, the way they interpret and practice their own beliefs. The ugliest and most arrogant attack on my own faith came at a retreat on Jesus led by a group of therapists claiming to base their teaching on a statement taken out of context from a letter of Carl Jung, of all people. If you didn't believe their interpretation of the New Testament, you were condescendingly informed you were simply mistaken (and probably not very bright).

Ironically, those Bible-interpreting therapists were the most intolerant religious people I've encountered, while the greatest message of tolerance I've heard came from a Roman Catholic monk. Father Nicholas Morcone, abbot of the Benedictine monastery Glastonbury Abbey, in Hingham, Massachusetts, said in a homily he had trouble reconciling the views of God in the lessons he had read that day from the Old and the New Testaments in his lectionary. He admitted he had been confused before by conflicting images of God in the Bible, and he had come to believe that "we must take God as he comes to each of us."

That is the spirit in which I offer my Spiritually Incorrect Outlook in the pages that follow.

3

Hearing Voices

We usually think of a spiritual path as one that will lead us to peace and harmony, bless us with serenity and contentment. Dealing with the pressures of daily life, from the emotional to the financial, as well as the demands and challenges of the world in the hyped up, super-techno twenty-first century, many of us look to religion and spirituality for comfort and guidance. Whether we belong to a church or synagogue, or follow any formal religious belief, many of us practice disciplines like yoga and meditation, or take workshops and go on retreats seeking enlightenment as well as greater balance in life, a deeper sense of well-being.

Any serious practitioner knows that such hopes are often fulfilled, to a greater or lesser degree; yet we sometimes fall into a kind of spiritual complacency, an illusion that religion or spirituality is by nature a source of solace. We forget that sometimes, in the wise words of an old Yiddish proverb, "God is an earthquake, not an uncle."

What provoked these thoughts was the observation of a psychiatrist on dealing with patients who have extraordinary religious experiences, such as seeing visions or hearing voices. Monica Grygiel, a psychiatrist described in a *New York Times* article as "a person of faith," said, "I experience my great poverty before the Mystery perceived in the religious experience. My hope is that I will not destroy the patient's extraordinary experience, but help him or her integrate it into the rest of life as harmoniously as possible."

I admire as well as respect Dr. Grygiel's humility in the face of Mystery. It is a welcome relief from the former dismissive attitude of orthodox psychiatry toward anything religious, an attitude established by Freud when he wrote about the subject in *The Future of an Illusion*. In 1994, the American Psychiatric Association officially declared that religious or spiritual experience was a normal part of life, and more therapists are dealing with it from such a perspective.

Despite the benevolence and good intentions expressed by Dr. Grygiel, I wonder if spiritual experience can always be "integrated" into one's life, especially in a way that's "harmonious." How would Joan of Arc have integrated into the rest of her life in a harmonious way the voices she heard that told her to put on armor and lead her country into battle? Her father had wanted her to stay home, which surely would have been a more "harmonious" course to take. But the Maid of Orleans listened to the voices and led France to its very identity as a nation.

What advice would the therapist have given Joan when she was brought before church officials who feared her power and influence and demanded that she deny her voices or be burned at the stake as a heretic? Surely denial would have been the most prudent course, the chance to return to her own village, as she wished to do, and live the rest of her days "harmoniously." Yet she could not deny the voices, the very source of her greatness, her identity not only to herself but also, as it turned out, to Western history.

What would the good psychiatrist have said to the young man named Francis in the town of Assisi who also began to hear voices? In *Francis: The Journey and the Dream,* Father Murray Bodo writes of "the patterns of highs and lows" in the life of the future saint. Perhaps Francis was bipolar. Wouldn't he today be prescribed some mood-altering drug after reporting that he had kissed a leper? A voice told him to leave the papal armies he had joined and return home, where he was scorned and branded a coward. He heard the voice of Christ and begged in the streets, stripping off his clothes, wanting to give all that he had to the poor. Surely any good psychiatrist would have pointed out that he could be a good Christian and even serve the poor in a more conventional way, a way that could be integrated more harmoniously into his life. Yet the safer course would not have led to the work that made him one of the most beloved and inspiring of all the saints.

People hear voices in our time, too—and not just schizophrenics and the mentally disturbed. After four children were murdered in the bombing of a black church in Alabama by racists trying to stop the burgeoning civil rights movement, Dr. Martin Luther King Jr., wondered if he should carry on the fight, if the death of innocent children was worth it. He got on his knees in his kitchen and prayed for answers, and he heard the voice of Jesus, telling him to go on, to continue his work. Surely he could have soft-pedaled his work, pulled back a bit, as so many wanted him to do. But he obeyed the voice and took the path that led to his own assassination, yet altered the course of life in this country.

Inner voices may be confusing or self-destructive or even satanic, as in the case of the notorious American serial killer called the Son of Sam who said he was "told" to carry out his murderous acts by a neighbor's dog. Not many of us are destined to become saints or to change the course of history, yet we all face decisions, and sometimes even hear voices, or inner promptings, that indicate a particular course of action. We are wise to listen to psychiatrists as well as to religious advisers, yet in the end we must make our own decisions. As Father Bodo says in writing of St. Francis, "To listen to one's own heart when others are saying something different is the hardest test of one's spirit."

Sometimes the most harmonious course may not be the right one. Sometimes we may not be able to integrate the message of an inner voice into our life but, rather, must follow its direction to discover a new life that may be more uncomfortable, even more dangerous. It may also be the voice of our deepest self, the one that leads to our true destiny.

4

Is Poverty Sacred, Wealth Profane?

Whatever happened to the notion that one can "do well" by doing good?

Why is it that if you are doing good work that helps other people, you aren't supposed to be paid well, if at all?

In a society that equates earning power with prestige, where money is regarded not only as the goal but the grail, it seems ironic—as well as unfair—that men and women who are engaged in work that nurtures the body, mind, and spirit are often looked upon with disdain if they profit from their efforts.

A case of this puzzling paradox came up recently as part of the internecine conflicts within the yoga community—a fascinating world with its own intrigues, divisions, power struggles, guru rivalries, and gossip. Whether we like it or not, all of those disturbing elements flourish in a spiritual context as abundantly as in any corporate, academic, or political arena. Just ask any priest, rabbi, or minister about the factions within their own congregation.

The yoga practiced in this country is primarily Hatha yoga, the yoga of the body, which by its very nature is a form of moving meditation. Some teachers, however, give it a more overtly spiritual context, by chanting *Om* before and after class, using incense and candles, and concluding with folded hands, a bow of respect between teacher and students, and closing with the Sanskrit word *Namaste,* meaning "I honor the light within you."

Upsetting the balance and serenity that yoga strives to create, one yoga teacher recently charged that another, who teaches the form that the first one pioneered, is "only money making." Eighty-five-year-old Pattabhi Jois, a star of the current yoga firmament, expressed his displeasure to journalist Rebecca Mead in her *New Yorker* article, "The Yoga Bums." Mead reports that Jois dislikes "other people making money from his system," and has a "particular animus" against his former pupil Beryl Bender Birch.

A popular yoga teacher in New York City and author of *Power Yoga* and *Beyond Power Yoga,* Beryl has made the Ashtanga method practiced by Jois accessible to Americans by recounting her personal experience with the form. The books use text and photos of the author and her husband, Thom Birch, doing the poses and explaining their benefits for our high-pressured lives. The books give full credit to Jois as a modern pioneer of the age-old Ashtanga method.

Jois learned the physically rigorous Ashtanga practice from his teacher, the Sanskrit scholar Krishnamacharya, who said he discovered the instructions in an ancient manuscript in a Calcutta library. (Jois says the manuscript was later eaten by ants.) Jois teaches the form at his studio in Mysore, in India, where increasing numbers of Europeans and Americans go to study. He also tours the United States, and the *New Yorker* reports that "he has found unlikely fame among the American upper middle classes and their entertainment gods."

In India, Jois charges Western students $500 a month to take his classes, which makes him a wealthy man in his native land, where the annual per capita income is less than $400. I applaud his popularity and prosperity, derived from teaching a difficult, disciplined, and rewarding practice to students of different cultures. What disturbs me is his charge that a fellow teacher's work is "only money making."

The accusation raises an old question of why people who do work that helps other people—especially if it has spiritual overtones—are not supposed to profit (or at any rate not make more than enough to get by). "It's interesting that we say it's all right for people to 'prosper,' but not to 'profit,'" says Beryl Bender Birch. "We're supposed to have 'abundance,' but not supposed to make money."

I took Beryl Bender Birch's classes when I lived in New York from 1992 to 1994 and got to know her and her husband and teaching partner, Thom Birch. They aren't rich and aren't ever likely to be. Like most yoga teachers, they live modestly and moderately, wanting the common comforts most of us do. They are superb teachers—the kind who make you feel comfortable with your own ineptness and inspire you to continue a difficult and strenuous practice. Their work enlivens, strengthens, and inspires people, and they deserve to make money for it. Too bad that, of all people, another yoga teacher who's become rich himself begrudges them making a living through their work!

As more people devote their lives to work that comes under the general heading of *spiritual* or *healing,* and more of us seek such teachers/counselors, the question of payment for such services has become increasingly relevant. A meditation teacher in California worries about the ethics of charging a fee for her work, yet as she devotes more time to it she is more dependent on reimbursement. Rather than setting a fee, she asks for a "love offering," hoping for the kind of pay a therapist might charge for an hour. To her disappointment, she is often given only $5 or $10. The givers think that's generous, but the teacher considers those sums more like a tip than a payment for services rendered. When I discussed the dilemma with my friend, Reverend Carl Scovel, he said this teacher needed to be more frank about her needs: "Putting a fruity name on it [her fee] only compounds the problem."

More and more spiritual directors, whose counsel on prayer and meditation inevitably crosses over into the realm of therapy, are also beginning to face the issue of fees. Most who are on the payroll of a church, religious order, or institution don't charge a fee, but may ask for a contribution to their supporting group. Those who work independently must determine, like the meditation teacher, a fair charge for services rendered.

Another minister friend told me his rule is never to charge for any services provided to members of his congregation, but for outsiders he asks $200 to perform weddings or funerals (involving preparation time and an afternoon for the event). "I made the mistake of not asking a fee from someone I met at a twelve-step program," he said, "but simply asked for a contribution. He gave me $25, and I felt like telling him he must need it more than I do."

The lesson seems to be this: ask a fee, and it shall be given to you; otherwise expect no more than a pittance. I recently paid a computer expert $75 an hour, which seems to be the going rate in large cities. Does a yoga teacher, spiritual director, or meditation teacher deserve less?

5

A Vote for Women
as Ministers

When I was recently back in my hometown I read on the front page of the *Indianapolis Star* that a twenty-nine-year-old local woman (originally from Texas) was a leader in the movement to oppose the ordination of women in the Southern Baptist Convention, the largest Protestant denomination in the United States, with more than 15 million members nationwide. The resolution passed as expected at the denomination's convention in Orlando, though the controversy over women as pastors is one of the key issues that led to formation of the Cooperative Baptist Fellowship, whose congregations take a moderate stand on that and other theological issues.

The young Indiana woman I read about, Heather King, is a lifelong Southern Baptist who felt a calling in high school to serve God. She earned a degree in biblical studies, took counseling courses at a Baptist seminary, and has worked ever since with women in Baptist churches throughout Indiana to develop programs in evangelism and spiritual development. She told the *Star* that Southern Baptists "have always affirmed the spiritual gifts of women" but believe Scripture teaches that the role of pastor "is limited to men."

King sounds like a sincere and dedicated woman, and I respect her service to her church as well as her beliefs, which I may disagree with. I was prompted to comment on her campaign opposing women's ordination because of the coincidence (or is it synchronicity?) that she lives in the place where I came to believe that women *should* be ministers. I was nine years old.

I first met Amy Franz even earlier, when I was baptized as an infant at the First Presbyterian Church in Indianapolis, and I first remember her as my Sunday School teacher when I was five. Amy was a warm, round, apple-cheeked woman with her gray-black hair pulled back to a bun, and she wore rimless glasses. In my memory she is wearing a dark red dress and those black, lace-up, square-heeled shoes that used to be standard gear for lady schoolteachers.

I also have a vivid memory of a painting that hung in Amy's Sunday School classroom, a picture of Jesus holding a child and other little children gathered around him. The faces of the children were all different colors—black, white, yellow, and red. That was an unusual sight in the 1930s in Indiana, which had the largest membership in the Ku Klux Klan of any state outside the South. Even more unusual was that Amy taught us that Jesus loved all these children, no matter what their color, and we should too. These and other radical ideas (straight out of the New Testament) led to a general feeling among the congregation that Amy was a little "touched," that is, slightly kooky. She had to be tolerated, though, because she was the minister's wife.

The minister was a tall, stern man with silver hair, whose voice was as deep and sonorous as I imagined the voice of

God. He was highly respected, if not universally loved, and as a child I felt a little afraid of him, in the way I'd be afraid of God (to whom I felt this minister bore a striking resemblance). He was pleasant enough to everyone in his formal way, but my parents and I would never have dreamed of going to him with our problems. Besides, he seemed more concerned with the important members of the church. It was Amy, his wife, who took in the strays, which included me and my family.

Around the time I was nine years old my parents began having difficulties with their marriage, and I was becoming more silent and sad around the house. If there were any psychiatrists in Indianapolis in 1941 we didn't know them, and if we had, we would never have dreamed of seeing them. We went to Amy because she seemed to love us rather than judge us, and the three of us felt so comfortable in her presence we could say things to her—and to one another—that we couldn't seem to say to each other at home. We had tea in Amy's sunny living room, a custom I thought was very English and special, and the tea, like Amy, helped us feel warm and safe. To me, Amy was the "real minister," while her husband seemed more like the figurehead of the church, his stern visage like those carvings of gods and goddesses on the bows of old ships.

We went to Amy's periodically all the way through my high school years, but it wasn't until much later, when I went back to church in my middle age, that I realized how crucial Amy's role had been to my family. She was our counselor, our healer, and, in the deepest sense, our minister. I know Heather King and the others who oppose women's ordination would argue that Amy did what she did in a role they'd approve, as a minister's wife; but I've since observed and experienced the kindness and sensitivity she conveyed in women who serve today as ministers and also as rabbis. In no way does this gift detract from their ability to preach, administer, and carry out the full range of duties as the leader of a congregation.

After all, the historic role of women as mothers and/or nurturers surely qualifies them for the mission expressed by Jesus when he said that he "came not to be ministered unto, but to minister, and to give his life a ransom for many" (Mark 10:45). No one is qualified to minister because of gender; by the same token, no one should be prevented because of it.

6

Spirited Pets

I n one of the darkest periods of my life, when my "resting pulse" was racing at twice the speed of normal and my personal and professional life was crumbling around me, my greatest source of comfort came from a cat.

I had not yet rediscovered my faith, and my relationship with the woman I lived with was in a near-the-end stage of paralysis. I was also near the end of my "Hollywood Period," brightly begun by creating the series *James at 15,* but drawing to a close with scripts turned down and pitch meetings that ended with the deadly phrase, "We'll get back to you." When I went home to slouch on the couch in the most discouraging times, Puss, the fat old cat, would appear, stare at me a moment, and jump on my lap, kneading my stomach and purring a sound of feline tranquility. She *knows,* I thought, and she *cares.* The idea that good old Puss the cat was trying to cheer me up was deeply reassuring, a kind of sustaining message that bridged the time before I hit bottom and found again the solace of the Psalms.

I experienced what countless people know from their own pets, that these domesticated animals possess a wordless wisdom, and convey or transmit a special kind of spirit that enriches our lives. The latest testimonial to this phenomenon comes from an old friend of mine, Helen Weaver, who has written and privately published a moving book about her communication with her own longtime pet, *The Daisy Sutra: Conversations with My Dog* (www.daisysutra.com).

Helen's professional credentials are quite solid. A literary translator, her translation from the French of *The Selected Writings of Antonin Artaud* was nominated for a National Book Award.

When she moved into her parents' house to care for her aging mother, she was told by a wise friend that the house was too big for its few occupants, and she needed a dog. At the local Animal Welfare Society, Helen picked out a "medium-sized black dog with white socks and belly," a shepherd with beagle and collie mixed in. She was your average, workaday pet, but, to Helen, the dog was special. "Once she turned her head toward me and I looked into her beautiful, expressive brown eyes, it was all over."

Wanting to train Daisy not to wander off the ten-acre property, Helen walked her along the boundaries several times, "telling her solemnly with voice, eyes and gesture, 'This is our land,' and 'This is not.'" Daisy learned the lesson so well, she refused to go with Helen to the mailbox, sitting down "at the exact spot where our property legally ended."

Though not trained to perform, whenever her leash was picked up to go for a walk, Daisy would "get up on her hind legs and dance and sing. The word *beagle* comes from the old French *bee gueule,* open throat, and beagles are the singers." Little wonder that Daisy soon became part of the family and Helen's great friend for sixteen years.

The usual story of a pet and its person would have ended when Helen saw that Daisy was too feeble to go on—a victim of the aging disease a friend of hers aptly dubbed "Dogheimers"—and decided to put her to sleep. But Helen had doubts about ending the life of her old companion. She heard there were people called "animal communicators" who can pick up the feelings of pets and who believe that "animals, like humans, have a spiritual essence that survives death."

A friend told Helen she had communicated with her cat through such a person both before and after the life of the pet, and Helen began her own "conversations with my dog" through several such professional communicators, first to be assured that Daisy was ready to die, and then that she was well and happy in the realm of her next life. The messages were not unlike the ones that humans receive from psychics about loved ones living and dead ("My body is weak. My spirit is strong and can be set free.... To know what it feels like to be without a body, think of joy").

Helen wondered if the animal communicators were "really channeling Daisy, or their own inner wisdom? I don't know, and I don't think it matters. What matters to me is that the words carried a precise personality and a boundless love that I recognized as real."

As indicated by the *sutra* in the title of her book, Helen is a Buddhist, but she quickly dismisses the well-known Zen koan (recently the subject of debate in *Tricycle: The Buddhist Review*) that asks: "Does a dog have Buddha nature?" Helen says, "To me it's just a stupid question that any Zen teacher should be ashamed to ask.... Everything that exists has Buddha nature." That's what Helen felt from her dog, Daisy, and what I felt from Puss the cat back in Hollywood—a love that wasn't dumb, but came from an instinct, an understanding of distress, and a wish to alleviate it.

It turns out there are dozens of books, tapes, and articles affirming that connection, including works by well-known authors such as Jane Goodall (author of *Reason for Hope* and *Gorillas in the Mist*), nature writer Farley Mowat, and psychiatrist Jeffrey Masson. Helen lists these resources at the back of her book, noting that new books on animals come out nearly every week, most agreeing that "animals are more intelligent and emotionally complex" than we believed—in other words, more like us.

Whether one believes that "talking to the animals" is possible, in life or in the hereafter, it's clear that more and more people are recognizing that animals are creatures of spirit as well as flesh and bones.

7

The Coffee House as Sacred Space

I t never occurred to me to question the name of my favorite coffeehouse in Miami, where I live now: the Sacred Grounds. Throughout my adult life, wherever I've lived, I've been lucky enough to have a coffeehouse in my neighborhood. I don't mean a Starbucks, which now seem to be in every neighborhood in the known world (a comedian quipped on TV that he heard Starbucks was cutting down on its expansion, which he thought might mean they were closing the one in his living room). I am talking about a category I think of as neighborhood coffeehouse, which by definition is not part of a chain, not a franchise operation, but a place unique unto itself and its environs.

My neighborhood coffeehouse, whether it was the Caffe Peacock in Greenwich Village, Il Dolce Momento on Boston's Beacon Hill, the Grove in San Francisco's Marina, the Cow's End in Venice, California, or the Sacred Grounds in Miami Beach, has served me as an office, meeting place for friends and business associates, site for interviewing or being interviewed, place for making notes and recording ideas, provider of physical nourishment in food and drink.

More important, I realize now, was its role as a haven

from stress, an oasis of comfort in being known and greeted as a frequenter, a place of relative quiet except for conversation and in some cases music. Coffeehouse music was usually classical and soothing, allowing you to read the paper or a book or simply sit and think, or muse, letting the mind wander without the pressure of time limits or requirements for spending or consumption—elements that nurture the spirit, enhance the soul.

I realized how important this was a year ago when I moved from my neighborhood in South Beach to Bay Harbor Island, twenty minutes north up Collins Avenue. My new neighborhood has restaurants, a shopping mall, a library, and even a well-known drugstore with a counter and booths for breakfast and dinner and snacks—but no coffeehouse. I tried the drugstore a few times but the staff was surly, the coffee lukewarm, and the ambience bland, so I soon found myself making the twenty-minute drive back to South Beach, just to go to the Sacred Grounds for my ritual coffee and scone. Of course, I could have gotten coffee and a scone at a number of places nearby, including the surly drugstore, but I couldn't get what I found at the Sacred Grounds—and what made it sacred.

This was a mom-and-pop operation, with a young mom and pop, Jackie and George, and a year or so after opening, they added to their family a lovely daughter named Isabella. Greeting Isabella and watching her grow and take her first steps was part of the homelike atmosphere, the personal warmth and spirit of the place.

There was nothing fancy about it, just a long narrow space with a display case of scones, pies, cakes, and bagels, a counter where the food and drinks were served, a sagging couch and low table opposite, and small round tables and chairs up front by the window. Paintings by local artists were on the walls, along with one large permanent painting of a coffee cup that was the symbol of the place, and that was pretty much it. The ambience came from the low-key, welcoming grace of the owners, the family, who never intruded or presumed on your privacy but made you feel at home, available for help or conversation or service if you needed or wanted any or all the above.

I knew they were having a hard time hanging on as South Beach became increasingly chic, popular, overrun, overpriced, and overfranchised. Rents and leasing fees were raised to make room for the likes of national names up and down Collins and Ocean Drive like Ben and Jerry's (replacing the Eighth Street Coffee Bar, another of the old-style coffeehouses), Johnny Rockets, T.G.I. Friday's, Banana Republic, Vidal Sassoon, and all the gang. Of course, there are also three Starbucks now in the neighborhood. I have nothing against Starbucks—they make good coffee, they even have tables and chairs—but they seem more suited to take-out or a quick snack, never for the kind of idling and daydreaming the old-fashioned coffeehouses encouraged.

I was out of town for three weeks this spring and when I got home, unpacked, and read the mail, I felt the need to get centered again, refocused, and the next day I got up early and drove in to the Sacred Grounds. There was brown paper taped to the windows; it was gone. I knew it was inevitable, but that didn't make it less sad, or the loss easier to fill.

I lament as well the increasing loss of its kind in the frantic franchisement of American life, the loss of individual, unique, local places with personal management and personality. After all, it was in the coffeehouses of Paris, like the Flor and the Deux Magot (which still thankfully flourish), where Hemingway wrote his early short stories, where Sartre and Beauvoir courted and held court. Coffeehouses were popular hangouts in the literary life of New York in the fifties, like the intimate Rienzi's, the spacious Limelight, the music-filled Figaro. Most recent of that vintage to close was the Caffe Peacock on Greenwich Avenue, with its heavy wood-carved tables and benches, the faded paintings of cherubs and saints, and slightly scratchy Italian opera playing from an old phonograph in the background. Coffee and scones were served instead of bread and wine, but these places offered their own communion. The spaces they provided of quiet and leisure in the midst of our cities' racket and rush were indeed sacred grounds.

8

Sexual Orientation
and the Spirit

Around the time of puberty, my childhood interest in formal religion—the churchgoing, Sunday School variety—began to fade. Looking back, I can see now that my yearning for God and spirit did not disappear, but shifted from indoors to outdoors, from church to nature, from choir music to birdsong and the music of water coursing over rocks and pebbles in running brooks (there was no ocean or lake in Indianapolis). The fiery rhetoric of the pulpit gave way to the wood fires I learned to make as a Boy Scout. Native American lore, with its awe of the Great Spirit, infused the scouting experience, beginning with the Cubs, in whose handbook I read the Omaha Tribal Prayer. On hikes with my troop, and at Chank-tun-un-gi, my much-loved Boy Scout camp, I sometimes felt the closeness to God that many young people find more movingly in woods and streams than in sermons and hymns.

Though scouting did not promote any particular religious belief, there was a sense of the spiritual in its principles of loyalty, respect, and service. The image of a Boy Scout helping an old woman across the street, à la Norman Rockwell, was perhaps a cliché of the sincere effort to instill in boys a value of helping those in need, and, hopefully, of growing up to be a Good Samaritan.

The spiritual aspect I found in my Boy Scout experience came to mind when I read about the Supreme Court hearing a case in which an Eagle Scout was kicked out of the organization because he was gay. James Dale is an Eagle Scout—as I was myself—who was serving as assistant scoutmaster of Troop 73 in Matawan, New Jersey, when a local newspaper ran an article about his also serving in the Lesbian/Gay Alliance. Because of that, he was booted out of the Boy Scouts of America.

Dale was told that the Boy Scouts "specifically forbid membership to homosexuals," though there is no such language in any of the Scout laws or oath or in the *Boy Scout Handbook*. The lawyer for the Scouts, George A. Davidson, argued that the policy of excluding gays was based on the Scouts' moral code, as expressed in the phrase "morally straight" in the Scout oath, and the word "clean" in the Scout law. The idea that homosexuality is a violation of such codes is becoming increasingly less prevalent as our society becomes more tolerant (as illustrated by the laws protecting gay rights), and more knowledgeable about human behavior, as expressed by the American Psychiatric Association's decision to drop homosexuality from its categories of mental illness.

While fundamentalist and other conservative Christians believe that homosexuality is prohibited by the Bible, most mainline churches now accept gay men and women as members. Those Christians who welcome gays to their congregations cite the example of Jesus in befriending and dining with those who were outcasts of society, in treating all men and women as brothers and sisters loved by God.

Dale, the fallen Eagle, felt he was fighting for the principles of scouting by exemplifying honesty, leadership, and standing up for one's own beliefs. His advocacy of honesty seemed to collide with the Scouts' position that only Scouts who had "publicly expressed their sexual orientation would face eviction." In other words, don't admit your sexual orientation and you'll be acceptable. Dale was not advocating homosexuality in the Boy Scouts, but asking only to continue his eleven-year scouting career, which the *New York Times* reported was, by all accounts, "exemplary."

Since the Supreme Court supported the Boy Scouts' right to exclude gays, I wish the Boy Scouts would look deeper into their own oath, their own laws, and see the spirit of brotherhood in them for all. It was more than fifty years ago that I earned the rank of Eagle Scout as a fourteen-year-old boy in Indianapolis, and I was told that "once an Eagle, always an Eagle." As an old Eagle now (not bald, but gray), I hope that boys coming of age today whose sexual orientation is different from that of the majority will not be excluded from the nurture I found as a Scout: the fellowship of comrades, the wonder of nature, and the lore of Native Americans who saw in sun and stars the evidence of Spirit greater than our own.

9

Is God in a Tree?

I eagerly awaited my first instruction from my spiritual director. I was a recently re-minted church member after twenty-five years of being away from any kind of religious practice, a layperson eager to "make up for lost time," and go deeper into the understanding of spirituality. My minister had recommended that I try spiritual direction, an age-old Christian discipline in which a seeker meets with a religious counselor to discuss ways of deepening prayer, trying to discern God's will, and become aware of how God is working in your life.

Now here I was at my first meeting with my newly assigned spiritual director, who, I was thrilled to learn, was a Roman Catholic nun. As a mainstream Protestant, I felt a nun would be able to fill me in on mysterious practices with beads and incense that would provide secret shortcuts and greater access to the Divine. My pen was poised and notebook ready for the nun's assignment that would surely introduce me to exciting, arcane practices.

"I want you to look at a tree," she said.

Is that all? I thought.

Maybe she thought that since I was a Unitarian, I wasn't capable of more than the simplest challenge. As it turned out, that became one of the most rewarding spiritual exercises I have ever done. The tree in fact looked too complicated for my beginner's contemplation and I chose instead a blade of grass to meditate on, as per instruction, for twenty minutes a day for two weeks, keeping a journal of the ways that God seemed manifested in what She created. Among the words I wrote were "resilient, tenacious, dancing, dependent, alive, reaching, responding."

That was the first of many lessons and experiences that enriched my life through spiritual direction, so I'm of course glad to see that the practice is becoming more widely known and available. Protestants as well as Roman Catholics and Jews are engaged in this practice, as well as seekers who may not have any church or synagogue affiliation but are trying to find their way to God.

Spiritual Directors International (www.sdiworld.org) lists members in thirty-two countries, with 4,148 in the United States, most of them Roman Catholic. Last spring I visited one of the new facilities offering spiritual direction among its programs when I gave a workshop at the Bryn Mawr Presbyterian Church's Middleton Center for Pastoral Care and Counseling in Bryn Mawr, Pennsylvania. The center's brochure explains that, in our present high-speed, high-tech life, many people want to explore the spiritual dimension, and satisfy the desire described in the Forty-Second Psalm: "As a deer longs for flowing streams, so my soul longs for you, O God."

While I was giving my workshop in Bryn Mawr, I met and talked with Gayle Kerr, one of the two spiritual directors on the Center's staff. She is a bright, personable, fifty-three-year-old woman with two grown sons, who studied five years to earn an M.A. in holistic spirituality, with a certificate in spiritual direction, from Chestnut Hill College in Philadelphia. Kerr sees twenty-five people a week individually in spiritual direction, as well as leading sessions in group spiritual direction, and retreats and courses on experiencing prayer. This work, she says, is "the joy of my life."

Kerr is one of those people who seems to genuinely radiate a quiet kind of joy, the kind that gives you confidence and trust. I could see at once why people would enjoy and benefit from meeting with her to explore questions of spirituality. The people who come to her seeking spiritual direction, she said, "want a deeper relationship in their prayer life, [have] a need to connect with God. Helping and guiding people with such purposes is wonderfully fulfilling.

"A woman I saw last night said, 'I have a hunger for God, I feel an emptiness I need to fill.' Some people come who aren't members of any church but are trying to find a way back to faith. Some feel their prayer life is 'dry,' or 'parched.' I see prayer as a relationship with God, and in any relationship, it's not all dramatic peaks and valleys; sometimes it's just plodding along—but that doesn't mean God isn't there."

Sometimes she suggests scriptural readings, psalms like 139, which eloquently shows God is always with us wherever we go ("If I make my bed in Hell, Behold, Thou art there"). She recommends Gospel stories of Jesus "showing compassion," and asks people in this process to read Scripture not for "information" like historical facts and figures, but rather for "*form*ation of our own souls.

"Some people come to spiritual direction hoping it's a kind of cheap therapy—they think it's easier than the hard work of building relationships. They think they can solve their problems just by praying harder."

When people come with personal problems that seem more in need of psychotherapy, Kerr refers them to one of the counselors on the Middleton Center's staff. "We have eight providers, including marriage and family counselors, and addiction counselors, as well as the two spiritual directors."

Kerr sees her directees twice a month at the beginning of their work, and then once a month after the basic relationship has been established. There is a sliding scale for payment from $30 to $50 a visit, though the Center offers grants for those who can't afford those costs, charging only a $10 administrative fee per visit.

Perhaps the most difficult part of spiritual direction is "discernment," helping people know God's will in making decisions, hearing "the still small voice" within. Kerr said one of her directees was torn between going on her church's trip to the Holy Land, which she felt an obligation to do but felt a knot in her stomach whenever she thought about it, or taking a sabbatical in New Mexico, which gave her a great sense of peace. "Go with the peace," Kerr always counsels. "Where the peace is, that's where God is."

10

Needed:
One Spiritual Emergency

When I came downstairs in my friend's house on Sunday morning on a visit to Boston, he looked up and gave me one of those mischievous Irish smiles and said, "It won't do you any good to go to that Protestant church this morning, Dan. You don't have a chance of getting into heaven." My friend Shaun is one of those "recovering Catholics" who does not harbor happy memories of growing up in the church, but is liberally tolerant of my own Protestant church, so I wondered what had prompted his dire theological prediction—before I'd even had my coffee! In answer, he handed me an article in that morning's *Boston Globe* called "Only Catholics Need Apply."

Paul Wilkes, the author of many well-regarded books on Roman Catholicism, explained in the *Globe* that the recent document issued by the Congregation for the Doctrine of the Faith (and approved by the pope) "unabashedly" proclaims that "the church of Christ ... continues to exist only in the Catholic Church." Wilkes wrote that the document "not only assigns other believers—including Protestant Christian ones— second-class citizenship, but bars them from the gates of heaven, despite their most sincere intentions and good lives."

This news did not discourage me from going to a Protestant church that morning, nor did it send me rushing to the nearest priest in hopes of gaining the gates of heaven by an instant conversion. It did, however, bring to mind my own mixed experiences as a "plain Christian" (Protestant, of assorted lineage) with Roman Catholicism, which have ranged from profoundly inspirational to deeply disturbing.

At King's Chapel, the Unitarian church in Boston (with its Christian theology and monthly Communion service), we often went on retreats to Glastonbury Abbey, a Benedictine monastery in Hingham, Massachusetts. There we were made to feel at home, and those of us who wished to join the monks in their services of prayer in the chapel—and even to take part in their daily Eucharist—felt welcome to do so. Often some of our more Humanist-oriented members, who came with trepidation to such a Roman Catholic institution, left with such warm feelings of gratitude for the hospitality that they voluntarily made a contribution (unsolicited) to the monastery. Many of us Unitarian Christians, myself included, came to look upon Glastonbury as our spiritual home away from home.

The service of the Eucharist, or Communion, in which the bread and wine are taken, as they were at the Last Supper, is for me, as for many Christians, the most intimate and meaningful of the Church's rituals. The late Father Henri Nouwen, a Roman Catholic priest and theologian who was one of the most inspirational of speakers and writers, and a friend in my own spiritual life, once gave me for Christmas a privately printed meditation he had written on the Eucharist, describing it as "the most ordinary and the most divine gesture imaginable."

While living in Boston in the 1980s I learned that there was a daily Eucharist service at the Paulist Center, and I began to attend. After participating several times, I thought that out of courtesy I should ask one of their priests if it was all right for me as a Protestant to take part. The Paulist Center was known as one of the most liberal of the Roman Catholic institutions in the city—one that was sometimes involved in controversy with the local cardinal because of its liberal positions—so I assumed there was no problem in my taking Communion there. Nevertheless, I wanted to show respect by asking.

Over coffee with a Paulist priest I had met once at a social event, I was told that in fact I was not welcome at their Eucharist: "Communion means 'community,' Dan, and it is not really appropriate to participate here if you are not part of the Roman Catholic community."

I'm sure my expression betrayed the shock I felt, and the priest added, "However, you may feel free to come if it's a 'spiritual emergency.'"

A spiritual emergency!

I thanked him for the explanation, apologized for my presumption, and wandered home in a theological daze, wondering who decided if I were experiencing a "spiritual emergency"? Did it have to go all the way to the Vatican? By the time my request had been considered and decided on, would the "emergency" have passed?

I am sure that if the judge were Cardinal Joseph Ratzinger, who issued the proclamation barring me from heaven, I would stand little chance of being okayed for Communion no matter how severe my spiritual emergency. I can only pray that my chances for heaven will rest on less restrictive standards.

11

Macho Men
at Prayer

The first time I ever heard a man who wasn't a minister, priest, or rabbi pray out loud, I felt so embarrassed and nervous I literally hid under the covers. I was attending a high school journalism convention, and my roommate, a friendly rival sports columnist on our school paper, the *Shortridge* (Indianapolis) *Daily Echo,* asked if I would like to join him in prayer.

We had each turned in for the night, and I was glad he had switched off the light before issuing his invitation, so he wouldn't see my panicked reaction. After I mumbled, "No thanks," I pulled the pillow over my head and lay there in frozen anxiety as I heard him say, in a clear, unaffected speaking voice, the words of the Lord's Prayer, and go on to express his love and concern for his family and friends, asking God's blessing of them. There was nothing bizarre or histrionic about my friend's prayer, yet it both awed and unnerved me, leaving an impression that has lasted half a century.

I still prayed sometimes in high school, though I wouldn't have wanted the other guys to know it. Saying prayers aloud seemed to belong to childhood ("Now I lay me down to sleep") and was the opposite of what we growing boys were trying to prove ourselves to be at age sixteen, which made my friend's spoken prayer seem all the more threatening. I even squealed on him, reporting his prayer as a joke to the other guys, thus showing me to be macho and a regular person, in contrast to his oddball behavior. What struck me then as weirdness I interpreted in later years as integrity when that high school journalistic cohort, Dick Lugar, became a U.S. senator from Indiana (and has proved that integrity time and again during his distinguished legislative career).

Of course, I felt hypocritical for making fun of Lugar's prayer in high school, while I continued to pray in secrecy and silence myself. Though I assumed most of the young men I knew then believed in God, even the star athletes and class officers, there seemed something weak-kneed or "chicken" about prayer, perhaps because we associated it with asking for help (which went against the manly Midwestern virtue of "pulling yourself up by your own bootstraps"). The main models we had of men praying (except for clergy) were the World War II heroes of the movies we grew up on.

Faced with a bayonet at the throat or a descending bomb while serving one's country, it was neither unmanly nor un-American to ask for help from a Higher Power. But once out of the foxholes (where, popular lore told us, "There are no atheists"), men returned home and changed from khaki into blue serge or gray flannel; they were supposed to "stand on their own two feet" and refrain from bowing their head except once a week at sanctioned services.

"Do you pray?" a man asked me at lunch in the executive dining room of his company. He had prefaced the question by saying, "I want to ask you about something," and warned a colleague of his at the table with us: "Now don't you laugh at me!"

When I answered "Yes," my interrogator followed up by asking, "When you pray, do you ever feel you are in touch with something beyond yourself?" I felt like a witness facing Perry Mason, and I wanted to answer as accurately as possible. "Sometimes I do, and sometimes I don't," I said.

The man eased back in his chair and said he hadn't ever experienced that feeling, though he'd tried to pray. We talked about it a little more, but he had satisfied his curiosity. I was struck by his sincerity, and his difficulty in raising the subject, an uneasiness I think common to most of us American men.

The women in a prayer group I belonged to at my church in Boston told me they thought men had a harder time with prayer than they did, attributing the difficulty to a quality that prayer required, one that they felt most men didn't possess or try to cultivate: humility. This explanation had never occurred to me; my own humility-consciousness was raised on the spot.

Since people know I have returned to church and write about spirituality, I've sometimes been called on to say a prayer to open a meeting, or grace before a meal. I still feel awkward doing it, with a sense of what seems like the old high school embarrassment. Worrying about the varying beliefs or lack of them among one assorted group that gathered for dinner and asked me to say grace, I couldn't think of any appropriate prayer, and as the tension and silence grew, I blurted out, "In the words of Tiny Tim, 'God bless us every one!'"

The best prayer I've heard from a layperson was offered at the Men's Immigration and Naturalization Service Detention Center in Boston. A dozen men from throughout the world (Sierra Leone, Pakistan, and the Dominican Republic were among the nations represented), who were trapped in a legal limbo, sat around a table in the bleakest of rooms. Reverend Constance Hammond, an Episcopal minister who had made this her parish, called on a handsome young fellow from Ghana to offer a prayer before beginning a Bible study session. Without any bumbling or hesitation, he boomed out in a joyous voice:

"Dear God, we thank you for giving us this wonderful chance to study your Word—help us to understand, give us much to put under our hat!" I smiled, and responded without my usual self-consciousness, "Amen!"

12

Speaking in Tongues

More than three decades ago, Harvard theologian Harvey Cox wrote a book called *The Secular City* in which he "tried to work out a theology for the 'post-religious' age that many sociologists confidently assured us was coming," a view that seemed culturally verified by *Time* magazine's famous "Is God Dead?" cover story. *The Secular City* became an unexpected best-seller and a kind of bible for a new generation of theology students and clergy who feared their own obsolescence in the coming "post-religious" climate, and found a rationale for relevance in Cox's book. In a recent book, *Fire from Heaven: The Rise of Pentecostal Spirituality and the Reshaping of Religion in the Twenty-first Century,* Cox announces, "Today it is secularity, not spirituality, that may be headed for extinction."

This will not come as a shock to readers of Cox's books, from his first vision of the secular city to his account of fire from heaven three decades later that completes his mapping of contemporary religious geography. In the intervening years he has brought us firsthand accounts of the shifting spiritual landscape, and its broader social and political meaning. He went south to support and write about the role of the black churches in the civil rights revolution and the movement's effect on his own faith *(Just as I Am)*, journeyed to Latin America to bring us news of the grassroots liberation theology movement that challenged the Catholic hierarchy as well as the political status quo *(The Silencing of Leonardo Boff)*, studied Zen Buddhism to trace the appeal of the Asian religions to America's young generation *(Turning East)*, dipped in the nude baths at Esalen as he reported on the spread of New Age influences on spirituality *(Seduction of the Spirit)*, sat in Hindu temples and Muslim mosques to explain the revival of religious power in other parts of the world *(Many Mansions)*, and wrote from his own experience about an interfaith marriage and family *(Common Prayer: Faith, Family, and a Christian's Journey Through the Jewish Faith)*.

Academic theologians have attacked his work as not being scholarly enough; he has breached the professional code by writing in an accessible way and thus has been branded a "popularizer." The stigma was reinforced at the teaching level when his course called Jesus and the Moral Life became the most popular undergraduate course at Harvard, drawing a thousand students to multimedia lectures in Sanders Theatre with gospel music pulsing while slides of Chagall paintings of Christian and Jewish symbols flashed on a screen overhead.

Cox has been criticized for not being a "true theologian" so much as a "theological journalist," a description that, in fact, best sums up his approach. Though it may be put down in academia, this method is regarded as admirable by those who believe there is value in experiencing a subject, getting to know the people who are living the story, and hearing about it in their own words. Being a kind of "George Orwell of theology" is not such a bad role, and Cox plays it with verve as well as integrity.

This is the method Professor Cox uses in *Fire from Heaven,* his book on the Pentecostal movement—the fastest-growing and perhaps most widely misunderstood religious faith of our era—not just as a phenomenon in itself but as one of the prime indicators of a religious renaissance Cox sees around the world:

> *Religions that some theologians thought had been stunted by Western materialism or suffocated by totalitarian repression have regained a whole new vigor. Buddhism and Hinduism, Christianity and Judaism, Islam and Shinto, and many smaller sects, are once again alive and well.*

Pentecostalism alone is growing at the rate of 20 million new members a year, with a worldwide membership that's reached 410 million. The Yoido Full Gospel (Pentecostal) Church in Seoul, South Korea, the largest of the world's mega-churches, has 800,000 members.

The most common misunderstanding of Pentecostalism is the outsiders' equation of it with fundamentalism. Cox stresses that "they are not the same. Fundamentalists attach such unique authority to the letter of the verbally inspired Scripture that they are suspicious of the Pentecostals' stress on the immediate experience of the Spirit of God.... While the beliefs of the Fundamentalists, and of many other religious groups, are enshrined in formal theological systems, those of Pentecostalism are embedded in testimonies, ecstatic speech, and bodily movement. But it is a theology, a full-blown religious cosmos, an intricate system of symbols that respond to the perennial questions of human meaning and value." It is based on direct religious experience, and therein lies its personal appeal and power. A favorite saying of Pentecostals is this: "The man with an experience is never at the mercy of the man with a doctrine."

The name *Pentecost* in Christianity refers to the New Testament account of the spirit of God infusing the followers of Jesus after his death to empower them to carry on his work. The event occurred in Jerusalem on a Jewish holiday that occurs fifty days after Passover (*Pentecost,* from the Greek word for "fiftieth day"). The phenomenon was marked by the apostles "speaking in tongues" (called glossolalia), seeing flames over the heads of those speaking, and, out of this experience, creating a new community that brought together previously divided languages and nations.

Pentecostalism has succeeded today, Cox believes, "because it has spoken to the spiritual emptiness of our time by reaching beyond the levels of creed and ceremony … into what might be called 'primal spirituality,' that largely unprocessed nucleus of the psyche in which the unending struggle for a sense of purpose and significance goes on." For Pentecostals who experience the trancelike state that leads to speaking in tongues, the experience is so total that, in Cox's phrase, "it shatters the cognitive packaging," breaking the barrier between the cognitive and the emotional sides of life, between the conscious and unconscious strata of the mind.

Cox reports that "Pentecostals began as rebellious antagonists of the status quo, refusing to serve in the armies of this fallen age, but many have now become impassioned super-patriots, easy marks for the high rollers of the religious right. They started out as a radically inclusive spiritual fellowship, in which race and gender discrimination virtually disappeared. That is hardly the case, at least in most white Pentecostal churches, today....

"I began to harbor the sad suspicion that the Pentecostal movement I had come to admire in my reading of its history and in my visits to other continents might be destined for an endless splintering into mean-spirited factions headed by power-obsessed egoists in the country of its birth. I feared that it might lose touch completely with its humble origins and become the righteous spiritual ideology of an affluent middle class."

Cox found the hope for the Pentecostal tradition he admired only forty minutes from his own Cambridge doorstep, in the Grove Hall section of Dorchester in Boston, an inner-city neighborhood so troubled it is known as Beirut West. A small congregation of young black Pentecostals, many of them graduates of the elite universities of the Boston area (the minister recruits at Harvard, MIT, and Boston University), have chosen to return to live in the ghetto as an expression of their Christian faith. They meet, pray, and sing in a rented hall, and help their parishioners and neighbors by attending court, monitoring police stations, training youth in work skills, and encouraging them to stay in school. They call themselves the Azusa Christian Community, adopting the name of the first Pentecostal church. "Never had I felt closer to the original spirit of Azusa Street," Cox writes.

With his usual approach, Cox went into the field as a personal observer/participant to write this story, which took him to four continents. Within the United States alone he attended services in seven different languages: "I worshipped with black, Latino, Anglo, and Asian congregations and started to sense a special closeness and affection for Pentecostal people." His own spirit of liberal commitment and humanist values infuses the book, reminding us that Pat Robertson is not the only kind of Christian.

13

New Age,
New Opportunities

O God, how manifold are your works ... in wisdom
you have made them all....

—Psalm 104:24

A few years ago I met a young minister who told me he
was fearful that members of his congregation were
being lured away from the true religious path (the
way of the Church) by the glamour and seduction of "New
Age practices." I was curious what specific interests his
parishioners were involved in—had they taken up crystal-
gazing? Were they listening to channelers with messages
from ancient Ptolemaic seers, transmitted in sepulchral
tones? What, exactly, had caught their spiritual fancy?

"Meditation," he said.

I was more startled than if he had said his parishioners were
into fire-walking. What was controversial about meditation? It
seemed to me that the notion of parishioners who wanted to sit
still and be quiet for a period of time would be welcome to a minister, under any name at all. The term *meditation,* though, refers
to one of the frequently practiced forms of a popular, contemporary discipline available outside of churches and synagogues, and

is associated with Eastern religious practices. That alone makes it suspect to many as alien and dangerous.

There is also, it turns out, a similar form of contemplative practice that began in the second or third century in the Christian tradition, according to Father M. Basil Pennington, the Trappist monk whose book, *Centering Prayer,* provides a contemporary guide to such practice. I read and learned from the book, and had the pleasure of interviewing Father Pennington, who teaches centering prayer throughout the world. He explained that *centering prayer* is simply a contemporary term for the form novice monks learned as the "prayer of the heart," similar to the form described in the spiritual classic *The Cloud of Unknowing.*

The twenty-minute practice of silence is comparable to meditative techniques like Transcendental Meditation (TM), an emptying of the mind to stillness. Instead of TM's use of a Sanskrit word or meaningless sound as a mantra, Father Pennington's method uses a loving word like *God* or *Jesus* to return to when thoughts distract and pull attention from the silent "center" of being. The period of silence in centering prayer ends when a leader quietly begins a spoken prayer like the Lord's Prayer, and others join in.

Basic, age-old practices being introduced to the lay public through alternative avenues of spirituality don't have to be a challenge to or diversion from either church or synagogue, but an opportunity to refresh, enliven, and strengthen one's own religious faith. The fear and apprehension stimulated by the very term *New Age* prevents some religious leaders from seeing unique opportunities.

"'New Age,'" Father Pennington said, "is a label for anything you don't like."

Fears of spiritual practices that originated in another culture are often stimulated by the press. Most journalists adopt a pose of jaded cynicism, whether about New Age spirituality, or, indeed, anything religious that might be taken seriously in public life—a point that is powerfully documented by Stephen Carter in *The Culture of Disbelief.*

The press leaped howling onto Michael Lerner's call for a "Politics of Meaning" in *Tikkun,* the excellent liberal Jewish magazine he edits, when it caught the attention and admiration of Hillary Rodham Clinton. Rabbi Lerner was described as a "Torah-thumping" journalist (suggesting he must be some kind of fanatic) in the *New York Times Sunday Magazine,* and labeled by the *Wall Street Journal* as "an aging '60s radical who still sees only a Government of the Good." Quoting from Lerner's editorials as well as a speech by Hillary Clinton, the *New Republic* jibed, "It's good to know the First Lady is pro-meaning. But before signing on, one question: What on earth are these people talking about?" In a later issue the magazine announced it was "still mystified" by Hillary Clinton's "spiritual quest."

As Father Pennington noted in speaking of journalistic antipathy to New Age movements or activities, "It's tragic the way the American press works, accenting the negative and eliminating the positive." This is an ecumenical point that dedicated seekers of all faiths might agree on.

I feel especially passionate about the distortion and dismissal of concepts labeled as New Age because I have gained so much, and my own faith has been so supported and deepened by courses, workshops, and teachers regarded as part of that realm. In a time of personal darkness, when the kind of prayer I had been practicing for ten years suddenly seemed shallow and mocking, I found in the silent physical movements of yoga practice a still point of faith and sustenance. In the much-maligned est training of Werner Erhard, which I found to be not a cult but a way of empowering my own faith, my long struggle with alcohol was resolved. In Zen "sitting" I found a way back to Christian prayer.

At the Esalen Institute in Big Sur, California, I discovered a deeper appreciation of nature and an understanding of mind-body-spirit through programs like the Aikido workshop led by George Leonard, a former *Look* magazine writer and editor who dropped out of establishment journalism to become a leader of the human potential movement and a black belt in the martial art of Aikido at age fifty-two (he was still hurling people around and being hurled himself in that practice in his seventies).

I have also enjoyed giving my own workshops in Spiritual Autobiography and Releasing the Creative Spirit at centers like Esalen; the Omega Institute in Rhinebeck, New York; and the New York Open Center, as well as houses of worship such as Marble Collegiate Church in New York, Fourth Presbyterian Church of Chicago, the Unitarian-Universalist General Assembly, the Paulist Center in Boston, Auburn Theological Seminary in New York City, and Temple Emanuel in San Francisco.

I have been moved by the sincerity and dedication of seekers of all faiths, not only those in Christian and Jewish congregations, but those without a church or synagogue at adult education centers, whether New Age or simply community-based, like the Boston Center for Adult Education. People who come to such workshops are seeking a way, a path, an entry to a spiritual dimension in life, and for some it may lead back to their own Jewish or Christian heritage, for some to Buddhism, or other Eastern faiths. In serving these people, as well as in exploring other ways of faith commitment along with them, led by others, I have never felt my own Christianity challenged, but, rather, enhanced.

I'm shocked sometimes at what seemingly innocent practices seem to terrify mainstream citizens—not just religious leaders. I was once invited to give my workshop in Spiritual Autobiography at a conference center in the South, and then uninvited when the center's director learned that crayons are used in one of the exercises in the workshop. This was "too far out," he told me.

The crayons also eliminated the chance to give a Spiritual Autobiography workshop for a business group in Boston on the grounds that using Crayolas made the program sound "too touchy-feely." That term is even more damning than the dreaded *New Age*. My proposal to write an article on the work of Father Henri Nouwen, the Dutch theologian who was pastor of the "L'Arche" community called Daybreak in Toronto (where volunteers live with and care for mentally handicapped people who would otherwise be placed in institutions), was turned down by a national magazine on the grounds that Father Nouwen's work sounded "too touchy-feely." Maybe because he helped a handicapped man get dressed every day, which involved touching.

If the mainstream press is so unnerved by spiritual subjects and practices outside of Sunday services, you may be wondering how such things can be successfully incorporated into the life of a mainline church—if they have any place there at all. Reverend Carl Scovel, who for thirty-five years was pastor of the very Bostonian congregation of King's Chapel, cited on the Freedom Trail as "the oldest continuing pulpit in America," introduced me to meditation, silent retreats, a healing group, a yoga class, and, perhaps most important, the Religious Autobiography course that he originated.

Those eight Wednesday night sessions of Carl Scovel's Religious Autobiography course in the Parish House back in 1984—when I drew pictures with crayons for the first time since Public School #80 in Indianapolis—started me on my own writing about religion and spirituality. It is the model of the Spiritual Autobiography course I lead throughout the country.

I believe Reverend Scovel would agree, as I do, with the eloquently stated belief of Tilden Edwards, director of the Shalem Institute, that "a truly universal faith is free to discern the hand of God at work anywhere in God's world."

III

The Spiritually
Incorrect Body

I t wasn't until I was forty-eight years old that I really "got it" about the mind and body being inextricably connected—not to speak of the soul, which I didn't much speak of anyway before that late-blooming age. It took my body breaking down to make me realize the mind had some effect on it, and vice versa, as well as the acknowledgment that certain human experience and behavior could only be explained by the intangible but no less real element of life known as the soul. What else drew me back to church to fill that area of life I had so long shut off?

I don't think it's an accident that my desire to go to church after years of scorning it arose during the first period in my adult life when I'd gone for more than a week without having a drink. This daring feat was accomplished out of stark fear when a resting pulse of 120 finally drove me to a program of exercise and diet that included going a month with nothing to drink at all—and saved my life from the premature end it was heading toward.

I'm convinced that numbing the body with excessive amounts of alcohol and/or drugs also numbs the soul, causing a kind of "spiritual blackout." When I cleared my body of the booze I had soaked it in for so many years, it seemed as if the spiritual impulse that was so long suppressed came shooting to the top of my consciousness. In New York in the 1950s I was told like others of my generation that to be a serious writer you had to be a serious drinker (writers as diverse as Pete Hamill, Joan Didion, and Norman Podhoretz are among those who have testified to this phenomenon).

We had bought the myth of "booze and the muse," so seductively glamorized by our generation's twin idols of literature—Hemingway and Fitzgerald. I don't remember anyone then who recognized—or was even aware of—the wisdom of Willa Cather on the connection of body, mind, and muse: "I try to keep myself fit, fresh; one has to be in as good form to write as to sing." Such an outlook was more difficult to live by and less darkly romantic than the Parisian hangovers of Papa and Scott, or William Faulkner's Southern Comfort. A boxer said once, "Kill the body and the mind will die." So will the soul.

Awareness of my body/mind relationship was brought home full force a few years after returning to church in a program I did that followed the old est training workshop of Werner Erhard, called the Six-Day Experience—a sort of est-ian version of Outward Bound. I took part in an exercise that required standing in front of a full-length mirror in nothing but your bathing suit with a few other participants, while the rest of the group looked on before taking their own turn. That was more challenging and difficult than the physical tests we underwent—running a mile uphill every morning; rappelling down a mountainside on a rope; climbing to the top of a thin, high tower and jumping off as you held on for dear life to a "zip line" that shot you into space; or being hooked to a rope that was stretched above a deep gorge and pulling yourself hand over hand to get across. None of that was as stressful as looking at your nearly naked body in a mirror. Some people cried.

The only reason I didn't cry when I stared at my spindly arms and flabby middle was that I was overcome with amazement and gratitude that this body had carried me as far and as well as it had, considering how little I had done for it and how much I had put it through. I had broken an arm and chipped off a tooth when I jumped off a fast-moving hay wagon in Israel, and I suffered a broken and dislocated fifth cervical vertebra from an automobile wreck after my junior year in college, spending three months in traction in the hospital, then three more months in a body cast that came over my head and down to my waist with a hole cut out for stomach and face, and another three months in a neck brace. For nearly a quarter of a century, I battered my body, mind, and soul with excessive booze consumption, added cocaine and LSD to the booze for a year in L.A. that I still am not sure how I lived through, ate whatever was greasy enough or sweet enough to satisfy a taste that can best be described as "prolonged adolescent gourmand," and indulged in no exercise greater than lifting cases of half-gallon jugs of wine in and out of the liquor store to take to my house. Somehow, despite all that abuse, the rather flimsy-looking body I was staring at in the mirror had carried me through a half-century! For the first time in my life, I was grateful to it.

I have managed to take better care of my body in the years since, but, like many of my aging, health-conscious comrades, I've learned that a reasonable diet and exercise can't necessarily prevent the breakdown of parts that come with senior citizenship (ugh—the term itself is enough to take ten years off your life). Yoga has played a big part in my mental and spiritual as well as physical well-being, bringing that blessed blanking out of the mind's trivia tape, providing rest and relief from the babble in the holding of a pose that requires the full focus of attention in all your vital parts.

The health spa Rancho La Puerta, to which I went first to write about in 1984 on assignment for *GQ*, and returned every year as a writing teacher and speaker to earn my stay, is as much a part of my spiritual journey as Glastonbury Abbey, where I always find spiritual rest and revival, healing of spirit and soul. I know these powerful places not only have enriched but also extended my life. I feel about my good fortune in finding them as I did when I told Reverend Carl Scovel how lucky I was to wander into his church that Christmas Eve. With a spiritually incorrect paraphrase of a line from *Casablanca,* I said, "Of all the gin joints in all the world, and I walked into this one!"

14

Many Roads
to Recovery

I never went to AA, but twenty years ago I underwent a lifestyle change that involved an exercise and diet program and a return to church and a spiritual path. From a daily dependence on alcohol that periodically turned into binge drinking, I went for long periods of abstinence to times when I have a glass of wine with dinner or at a social function or celebration.

My friends in AA still refer to me as an alcoholic, since I've never done the twelve-step program and still sometimes have that glass of wine. One evening over dinner I asked one of those AA friends if she'd mind not calling me an alcoholic, explaining that that isn't how I define myself, and I quoted the definition of alcoholism from my *American Heritage Dictionary:* "the excessive and habitual consumption of alcohol."

My friend wasn't comfortable with that definition and suggested that we call a doctor to get a medical definition. I said the dictionary definition was good enough for me, and if she saw it differently that was fine too. I simply wished she'd stop calling me an alcoholic. She suddenly said, "Screw it," picked up her purse and books, and stormed out of the restaurant.

One of the drinking buddies of my boozing days is an Irish fellow who stopped drinking twenty years ago and has never had a drop since, without the aid of AA, therapy, religion, or any self-help or spiritual program. His friends in AA lament that he is, nevertheless, what they call a "dry drunk." In my non-AA layperson's view, a drunk who doesn't drink is a contradiction in terms.

I have the greatest respect and regard for AA, which has saved millions of lives, and, as Kurt Vonnegut has said, may even turn out to be America's most important contribution to Western civilization, not only for helping people conquer alcoholism, but also for providing a network of "families" throughout the world in an era of social breakdown and isolation. My argument with the program is its insistence on being the *only* way to deal with the problem of alcoholism, and its views as the only legitimate ones on the subject.

An important book by the health and medical researcher Anne M. Fletcher, *Sober for Good,* shows that there are many routes to recovery, and the idea that Alcoholics Anonymous is the only way is a myth. Based on in-depth interviews with 222 men and women who were former alcohol abusers, Fletcher concludes that sobriety was achieved through a variety of paths and programs, including therapy (most notably cognitive-behavioral therapy, which helps people change their behavior by recognizing self-defeating thought patterns); programs such as Women for Sobriety, which stresses strength rather than AA's admission of powerlessness over alcohol; Smart Recovery, which emphasizes individual responsibility; and Secular Organizations for Sobriety, for those who don't accept the AA belief in a higher power.

Twenty-five people in Fletcher's survey of those who maintained sobriety for more than five years quit on their own, like my Irish friend, with statements like "I put the cork in the bottle" and "That's it, I quit." Among those Fletcher calls "masters" over alcohol—sober for at least a decade—a few have found they can drink moderately, and she concludes that "at least for some people, one drink does not a drunk make." Ninety-six of those surveyed achieved sobriety through AA, while the rest—a little more than half—took the variety of paths mentioned above.

The hopeful and valuable message of the book is that there are many ways to conquer abusive drinking, not just one. Of those who join AA, only 10 percent stick with it after a year, and it will surely be encouraging for the dropouts—and their loved ones—to know that there are other options, that they have not tried and failed the only course to recovery. Rick N., one of Fletcher's respondents who has been sober for twenty-one years, said, "There are probably as many ways to defeat alcohol problems as there are people who want to recover. The more choices we can offer, the more people can be helped."

15

When Prozac
Spells Relief

Q. *A recent cartoon in* The New Yorker *showed a woman telling a friend she's discovered there are times in a person's spiritual journey when prescription drugs are "entirely appropriate." The joke seems to be that people on a spiritual journey are copping out if they take prescription drugs. Is taking Prozac or similar mood-enhancing drugs regarded as spiritually incorrect?*

A. Sad but true! Recently, a friend who was suffering a deep depression told me she feared that if she followed her own doctor's advice to take Prozac, or one of its derivatives, it would mean she was not on the "Path." I strongly debunked this idea, quoting Reverend Theodore Ferris, a former rector of Trinity Episcopal Church in Boston, who said in a sermon, "Our faith is neither in pills nor in prayer. It is in God, who may use both pills *and* prayer as channels of his healing power." In an article called "The Gospel According to Prozac," in *Christian Century* magazine, Archibald Hart, dean of the School of Psychology at Fuller Theological Seminary, said that doctors prescribing drugs for the depressed "is no different than giving insulin to a diabetic."

Whereas most contemporary Americans are happy to credit medicine with curing their physical problems, many still feel demeaned by acknowledging medication as a cure for emotional problems. It seems especially uncomfortable for people trying to follow a spiritual path, as if the use of chemicals is "not fair" or that it's "cheating" to use medicine instead of—or as well as—spiritually correct techniques of prayer, meditation, yoga, or martial arts disciplines.

Carl Scovel immediately quoted Scripture when I asked him if he felt taking Prozac for depression indicated a lack of faith in the power of prayer: "Ecclesiastes 38:4. 'For medicines come from the hand of God and a wise man would not refuse them.'"

Rabbi Harold Kushner, author of *When Bad Things Happen to Good People,* told me, "If it's used to solve a particular problem, I totally approve—but if it's used because you feel good but you want to feel super, then I think it's wrong."

The fear of these drugs being used casually—because some-one just had a bad hair day—is a shared concern of most people of good faith. The counselors interviewed by *Christian Century* felt this medication should only be used for "severe" depression. California yoga teacher Paul Gould says, "There's use and abuse. But I do feel certain that for people with a chemical imbalance that Prozac can help balance out, it's a godsend. It can even help them see the spiritual path more clearly." His partner-teacher Jenni Fox agrees, saying, "You have to heal on all levels—you don't do medicine instead of other things but in addition to healthy practices like yoga and meditation."

Phyllis Pilgrim, longtime fitness director of Rancho La Puerta, who teaches a course there on the Inner Journey, feels people should first try natural remedies like St. John's Wort and ginseng "before leaping into drugs like Prozac," which she feels happens too often in "affluent America." But in cases of "a deep depression brought on by some serious trauma, Prozac could help."

To her surprise, Pilgrim found on a recent trip to Asia that doctors at Delek Hospital in northern India were using Prozac to help Tibetan refugees who had suffered deep phys-ical and emotional trauma from the six months of crossing the Himalayas into exile during the winter. "Even with the spiritual help these refugees get from Tibetan Buddhists," she said, "the doctors find Prozac helps their recovery."

In a time of my own depression, I took the Prozac deriva-tive Zoloft, on the advice of a Jungian therapist who is herself "on the path" of genuine spirituality. The drug's effect seemed to me a true blessing. It did not make me feel jangled or high, but, rather, simply lifted the depression and left me in a condition where I could function at my best and enjoy life. I am not presently taking it, but would not hesitate to do so if I fell into one of those pits of depression again.

I don't consider using such medicine as a sign of weakness or spiritual failure, but as a sign of a willingness to admit to a problem and pursue legitimate means to solve it. Putting down people who use such medication shows a kind of spiritual arrogance and self-righteousness. The best corrective to such negative attitudes is from James Baldwin's classic book of essays *Notes of a Native Son,* when he quotes a Harlem preacher: You can't judge a person *"if thou knowest not his wrassling."*

---- **16** ----

Soul Food?

Q. *I attend a meditation class every week at an adult education center, and recently some of us decided to go for dinner after class at a neighborhood restaurant. I was feeling hungry, and I ordered a steak. Up until that moment there had been a lively conversation at the table, but when I told the waiter I wanted a steak, the whole table fell silent. The others looked at me as if I had just said a bad word, or summoned the devil. One person coughed, and a few others looked away. The others ordered some kind of pasta or fish. Is eating a steak considered spiritually incorrect?*

A. Definitely! The Spiritually Correct Police will be on your case for eating any kind of red meat, but especially steak or prime rib, which are considered the most desirable (and usually the most expensive) cuts by meat lovers. Some of this antimeat attitude comes from people who feel that cows (and all other animals) are sacred. The most extreme of those who are vegetarians for reasons of principle rather than diet believe it is bad to kill and eat "anything with a face," which eliminates fish as well as chicken. I don't decry their position, but I don't think it makes them any more genuinely spiritual than people who eat meat, or frog's legs, or a piece of roast pork carved from a suckling pig with an apple in its mouth.

Many people associate meat with lusty, self-gratifying lifestyles, just as rice and vegetables are associated with discipline and denial. When I first went on a retreat at a monastery, I expected to sleep on a hard board, if not a bed of nails, and eat nothing but rice and tea, with perhaps an apple for dessert. To my surprise (and I confess, my pleasure) the meals at Glastonbury Abbey, the Benedictine monastery, were full and varied, including lasagna (with meat), roast beef, chicken, fish, pasta, and a variety of cakes and pies as well as fruit for dessert. This menu certainly did nothing to detract from the powerful spiritual aura of the place, the moving services of prayer, and the truly Christian hospitality of the monks.

Basically, the most "spiritual" diet is surely the one that keeps you the most healthy, in order to live to the fullest and serve your fellow humans. In recent years I have followed the diet that seemed to be the most spiritually as well as medically correct—the low-fat, low-protein, high-carbohydrate approach pioneered by such doctor-gurus as Nathan Pritikin and Dean Ornish, as well as government nutrition boards and the American Heart Association, featuring pasta, rice, fruit and vegetables, and, in modified form, including fish and even chicken (without the skin).

Now that is being challenged, most successfully by Barry Sears with the Zone diet, who declares in his best-seller *Enter the Zone* that "with these diets [low fat, low protein, high carbohydrate] we often get fatter even while following their guidelines with religious fervor." Sears wants us to eat nearly equal "blocks" of protein and carbohydrate—as well as some fat—but warns against carbohydrates with a high glycemic index, which means they turn into sugar and enter the bloodstream faster. Among these "unfavorable carbohydrates" are the very staples of the formerly correct diet: bread, pasta, grains, corn, potatoes.

According to the Zone approach, one of the foods most commonly regarded as sacred, in health as well as spiritual terms, turns out to be bad for us! Yes, friends, Sears warns that one of the rapid inducers of insulin (foods that have a high glycemic index) is, of all things, *rice!* Even more shocking, in the Zone view, brown rice is just as bad as white rice! If diet is religion, this is heresy.

With all the conflicting information and attitudes now going around about diet, we can only pray that we're eating the right thing.

17

Spa Spirituality

I've often said jokingly that I love the health spa Rancho La Puerta because it reminds me of Camp Chank-tun-un-gi, where I went in summers as a Boy Scout in Indiana. In fact, there are many true parallels in those experiences—not just the hiking and physical exercise, but also the sense of camaraderie, the community spirit that arises among people who in most cases haven't known one another before but have come to a particular place to engage in a similar enterprise with similar goals and values.

In the world of spas, this kind of community experience arises in the "destination spa," the kind where the clientele is there for a particular period of time, as at Rancho, where each session begins on a Saturday and ends the following Saturday. With the same group of people there for a week, there's time for a community awareness and spirit to develop.

Spa spirituality is usually thought of as the natural consequence of getting a healthy break from business and domestic duties and routines. People recharge the mind, body, and soul for the next challenges of life, aided by the kind of classes most spas today provide in meditation, and meditative disciplines like tai chi and yoga. Time for the nurture and nourishment of the self is the legitimate lure of a spa vacation. But rarely is community thought of as one of the benefits, either spiritually or socially. And at many spas it's not a factor.

Most people don't go to spas to meet people, either for social or mating reasons. The gender ratio of most spas is overwhelmingly female, so women don't go looking for a mate, but more likely see it as a place to relax from such concerns. The men who go understand—or soon learn—the women are not there to impress or please them, but, if anything, to take a break from all that.

Still, when men and women are in the same place, romantic connections sometimes occur. Digby Diehl, the writer and former editor of the *Los Angeles Times Book Review,* met his wife at Rancho La Puerta. On one of my trips there I met a woman with whom I carried on a bicoastal romance for several years, and I remain friends with her and her family, who are all Rancho returnees. But those cases are exceptions to the general rule.

The common experience of Rancho is meeting people just as they are, without pretension, makeup, or starch, sweating in sweatsuits and T-shirts and shorts, layered with dust from the mountain hike or sweat from the gym, sharing similar sensations of aching limbs, sore feet, and heavy breathing. You also see these same people transformed, emerging from showers, Jacuzzis, and saunas, smiling and fresh on the way to dinner. Unless you "vant to be alone," Garbo-like, or choose to only be with whomever you came with, you are seated at a big round table for six or eight, maybe all strangers before the meal, or people you met on the morning's hike or yoga class or circuit training.

Meeting in this informal way, eating and talking and hiking and exercising and learning together in a beautiful place, away from daily routines and responsibilities, creates a natural bond, possibly a quicker and deeper one than is likely to come in places where you always have to look your best, be careful about slipping up, be on guard and wary and protective. There is also the underlying, unspoken bond of choosing to come here, a place that some of your friends and fellow workers and maybe even family find superfluous or silly or boring or beside the point. There are people here you surely disagree with about religion or politics or ethics or aesthetics, but simply by being here you all share a faith in the value of what the place offers.

None of that needs to be spoken, and I realize that much of what I find spiritual at Rancho is not on the verbal level. There are no creeds or chants or liturgies; the text is in the rocks and flowers that border the hiking trails on Mt. Cuchama, shared by all who pass them in the day's early light; in the stretch of limbs doing the triangle pose in a yoga class, the crossed legs of those who come at noon to sit in the meditation room. None of this is done in isolation, not even the morning hike, for it's dangerous to go on the mountain by yourself, where snakes may be hiding and wildlife as well as cattle and horses roam. You are not alone as you reach for the sky in the Sun Salute to start yoga class, or rush from stationary bike to treadmill in circuit training; bodies of all shapes, sizes, genders, and hues are breathing and sweating around you, striving as you are, alone and together, under the same mountain, the same sun.

Communion is in the Silent Dinner held one night of each week at Rancho, when any who choose may sign up to go to a room with candles and music where all around the table agree to eat without speaking. You may smile or even laugh, make eye contact or simply concentrate on your food, but no words are spoken; you are alone to fully taste the food and be with your own thoughts, at the same time sharing this time and place and meal with others who are joined in a common enterprise, an exploration of sense and spirit. Afterward, there is an opportunity to speak about what you experienced, and that too deepens the bond of those around the table. This is a far different experience than eating alone in silence, just as prayer in community is different than praying alone, and provides an enriching sense of connection and support.

When I first became aware of the concept of a "spiritual path," I thought the highest, most desired form of spirituality was symbolized by the image of a lone monk on a mountaintop—the isolated holy man communing only with God. In the course of time and experience, I have turned 180 degrees to the belief that true spirituality is in community.

More than fifty years ago I enjoyed the community of other boys engaged together in outdoor physical activities at

Scout camp, where friendships were forged and our spirits lifted by a common sense of adventure, and of possibility. Now I go to Rancho La Puerta and find similar rewards of spirit as well as physical health, all of it enhanced by the sense of community, of shared experience. At dinner on the last night, addresses are exchanged with promises to meet on trips ("If you get to Seattle, you must—") or again at Rancho, some signing up to come same time, next year, to renew the newly made bonds. In seven days of shared activity a world is created, a spirit is born, and you take it home when you leave.

18

Does Yoga Make
You a Hindu?

An anonymous letter with no return address arrived at the home of Nancy Roth, an Episcopal priest and writer who leads workshops and retreats in Christian yoga. Reverend Roth was leading a retreat in another state, so her husband examined the letter, as one does in our age of anthrax, by holding it up to the light before opening it, to see if there were any clues to the contents. He saw the words *yoga* and *Christian*, so he thought it must be someone asking about her workshops. He opened the envelope to find a clipping from a publication whose identity was not included, denying the validity of Reverend Roth's recently published book, *An Invitation to Christian Yoga.*

"The clipping criticized my book, saying that yoga could not be 'Christian,'" Reverend Roth told me. "It 'warned' that yoga would inevitably lead people away from Christianity and put them in touch with Hindu deities. It was part of that whole fearful attitude of some fundamentalists."

Fundamentalist Christians aren't the only ones who fear that practicing the physical movements of yoga will mysteriously alter their belief system. I've met highly intellectual American atheists who fear that a yoga class that begins (as most do) with the chanting of *Om,* a universal breathing sound, was by nature "religious," and thus would corrupt the purity of their nonbelief.

I encountered the Christian fear of yoga when I went on a retreat in Mexico, and a yoga teacher from Mexico City said some of the Catholic priests there instructed their parishioners not to go to yoga class. They warned that the practice would lead to other gods and Eastern religious beliefs.

Though developed in the ancient Hindu tradition, the movements of yoga seem so universal that they can adapt to or be adopted by any culture or spiritual path. The great majority of classes in the United States teach the practice of Hatha yoga, the physical discipline that focuses on the postures or *asanas* of the ancient technique, and employ no religious teaching at all, unless you count the chanting of *Om* as a breath control to begin the class, and sometimes the teacher's blessing of *Namaste* at the end, meaning, "I honor the light within you." The "light" can be interpreted any way the student understands it, from the universal concept of spirit to the light of one's own faith, whether Christian or Buddhist, Muslim or Hindu, or simply "spirit" or even "science," or Freud or Jung or Oprah.

When Nancy Roth, a former dancer and dance instructor, took an adult education yoga class in her local high school thirty years ago (before she had entered the General Theological Seminary and become an Episcopal priest), she found the practice "a doorway to prayer."

"It did not matter that we had chanted *Om* or that the exercises had Hindu names," Roth writes in her *Invitation to Christian Yoga.* "My awareness of my own 'incarnated-ness' drew me closer to the Incarnate One. The One I encountered, as I lay on the gym floor with my body relaxed and my mind and spirit attentive, was the God I knew in Christ Jesus."

As a Christian and an Episcopal priest, Roth sees yoga as "the gift our brothers and sisters of another tradition have given us, as we strive to follow the way of the One who embodied God, Jesus Christ."

Roth's book is practical as well as inspiring not only for Christians, but also for others of no official faith who are open to the spiritual harmonies of the psalms and the Lord's Prayer. Selections from psalms that are appropriate to different yoga positions are suggested for meditation, and the Sanskrit names of the *asanas,* or postures, are given in English. For a meditation that might suit the posture of the Folded Leaf (also known as the "child pose"), Roth offers Psalm 131:3, "Like a child quieted upon its mother's breast, my soul is quieted within me." Lines from the Lord's Prayer are matched with the positions of the basic yoga posture Salute to the Sun, originally a practice of the devout Hindu for greeting the dawn.

While Reverend Roth puts the movements of yoga into a Christian context, the practice itself may be adapted to any spiritual path, or to none. *Yoga* means "yoke," or joining together, and what joins us as humans on a spiritual path is the recognition stated for Christians by Paul in I Corinthians 6:19, but applicable to all seekers:

> *Do you not know that your body is a temple of the Holy Spirit within you, which you have from God?*

IV

Profiles of Spiritually Incorrect Lives

Shortly after graduating from college at Columbia, I was lucky to stumble on spiritually incorrect institutions like the Catholic Worker and its Hospitality House in the Bowery, and the East Harlem Protestant Parish, a group ministry of young men and women who chose to live and raise their families in a poor and problem-plagued neighborhood. I found myself, a newly minted atheist-intellectual, admiring and even writing about such rare religious people whose lives really matched their faith. They led me to the neighborhood that became the setting and subject of my first book, *Island in the City: The World of Spanish Harlem.*

Throughout the following forty years, many of the people who inspired me then have continued to pop up again in my life and work, bringing new insights, leading me to new experiences and stories, renewing wonder and freshening faith. Reverend Bill Weber, one of the founders of the East Harlem Protestant Parish in the 1950s, turned up in my life again in the 1980s when he invited me to give my workshop in Spiritual Autobiography at the program he created for prisoners at Sing Sing to get a master's degree by studying theology. Since I'd seen him last, Bill had founded the New York Theological Seminary to enable more minority students to become ministers, chaplains, academics, and theologians, and launched the program for prisoners at Sing Sing. Now in his seventies, he continues to break old boundaries of "correctness," socially and politically as well as spiritually, proving that what cynics sometimes categorize condescendingly as "youthful idealism" isn't restricted to the young.

Such incorrectness wakes us up, makes us not only think but rethink our own ideas and understanding. The people who give us these wake-up calls may not be religious at all, or consider themselves spiritual in the narrow sense of the term that means a conscious (and sometimes self-conscious, or even pretentious) adherence to a religious faith or to certain physical and mental disciplines such as yoga, tai chi, meditation, diet, and workshops or courses of self-help or human potential. Our greatest awakenings may come from people we don't even consider—and who would not consider themselves—spiritual teachers or guides. Some of those people are included here—people like Werner Erhard, the controversial creator of est and the Forum; rebel sociologist C. Wright Mills; and "confessional" poet Anne Sexton.

Some of my most inspiring—and life-giving—surprises come from people and places I haven't considered in the realm of spirituality at all. Like Sports Radio. I never listened to those call-in shows where rabid fans rant, rave, and reminisce about their favorite teams and players until I came to Miami and spent some time driving a car instead of walking or taking cabs or subways, as I had when I lived in New York and Boston. Now I'm addicted to the radio shows of Hank "the Hammer" Goldberg and Jim "Mad Dog" Mandich on WQAM in Miami, which I turn to for entertainment, rather than spiritual insight or uplift.

I was happily surprised to find myself writing one of my Spiritually Incorrect columns based on the commentary of Hank the Hammer about the Miami University football coach Butch Davis. Davis claimed that the voice of God had told him to leave his college coaching job for a far more lucrative position in pro football. I laughed when the Hammer wondered if Butch Davis had seen any burning bushes on his lawn to affirm his sudden defection from the Miami Hurricanes to the Cleveland Browns.

I was astonished to find the only words that lifted me out of a postsurgical depression came not from my usual sources of spiritual solace but from listening to Jim "Mad Dog" Mandich on his call-in sports radio show. There are times when the old springs of spiritual refreshment seem dry, when the beautiful rhythms of the psalms sound more singsong than soothing, and the wise guides whose words you know and have always relied on ring empty and hollow in the mind. When my own state of personal despair after illness was driven deeper into depression by the attacks of 9/11 (I felt at the same time as if some interior Taliban had assaulted my prostate), it was not the sage wisdom of Thomas Merton or Rabbi Harold Kushner that broke my spell of despondency, but the words of Mad Dog Mandich.

For those readers who may be sports-challenged, Jim Mandich was an all-American football player at the University of Michigan and later starred with the Miami Dolphins team that made history with the only undefeated season in the annals of pro football. Now he is a successful businessman as well as a popular sports commentator. I enjoy Mandich not only for his insider's knowledge of sports, but even more for his genuinely upbeat attitude, expressed both in the positive timbre of his voice, and, more important, in the greetings he gives to callers who ask, as is the ritual on shows, "How ya doin', Mad Dog?" Most of the radio hosts reply curtly with quick clichés like "Doin' fine," or just a brusque "Okay," "Swell," "Alright," but Mandich puts feeling into such comments as "Never better," "The only way I'd be better is if I was twins," and "Life has been very good to me." On this particular day of my despond, a call came in from "Larry of Kendall," asking the traditional "How ya doin', Mad Dog?" to which Mandich's reply was "Larry— Every day's a holiday, every meal's a banquet."

The words of such genuine enjoyment of life broke through my miasma—the screen of self-pity that was shutting off any natural joy and pleasure—and I laughed out loud. My voodoo-like spell of self-pity was broken. I was free to feel good again. To laugh. To breathe.

I love those unexpected breakthroughs, the experience of being, as C. S. Lewis put it, "surprised by joy." Happily, it's impossible to contain the spirit in rules or dogma, nor can it be confined to beautiful cathedrals or even to breathtaking sunsets. Life-sustaining spirit may come to us from the pulpit or out of the mouths of babes, while lying on a yoga mat or driving down the interstate. God or spirit or whatever name you want to give to the life force breaks all the rules, is itself "incorrect." So are these people whose lives have lighted the way for others.

19

Who Do You
Think Is a Saint?

What makes a person a saint? And who gets to decide?

The questions came to mind when I recently read that Bishop Fulton J. Sheen, a prime-time television star of the 1950s, may become a candidate for sainthood in the Roman Catholic Church. The *New York Times* reported that the late Cardinal John J. O'Connor gave permission for a friar at St. Felix Friary in Yonkers to begin a study of the life of Bishop Sheen as the first step in the long process the Church requires for canonization.

I first heard of Bishop Sheen when I came home from Columbia College in the summer of 1954 as a proud intellectual atheist, and my parents insisted that I watch this TV priest. Bishop Sheen was outdrawing the era's hottest TV star, the comic Milton Berle, and had even won over my Midwestern Protestant parents, a breed congenitally suspicious of the papacy. Father Sheen shook up my smug atheism with a sermon on "The Hound of Heaven," the Francis Thompson poem about the man who fled God down the nights and down the days, but is caught by God in the end, as I feared might be my fate (a fate I would later welcome with open, broken heart).

I have often thought fondly of Bishop Sheen, and he has my vote for sainthood—but my vote doesn't count. I'm not even a Roman Catholic, and I'm not challenging the right of the Catholic Church to select its own saints, by its own methods, but I think the rest of us ought to be able to nominate and canonize our own saints as well.

That very idea has been carried out at St. Gregory's Episcopal Church in San Francisco, where a stunning mural above the altar portrays 81 men and women who have been chosen by a lay committee and clergy from a list of 350 names submitted by church members as candidates for sainthood. "We celebrate those whose lives show God at work," explains a document from the church, which fosters a broad idea of sainthood, rather than "the commonplace notion of rarified purity." The saints depicted include people of all faiths, some of whose names are as surprising as they are provocative: Ella Fitzgerald, Fyodor Dostoevsky, Anne Frank, and Malcolm X take their place alongside Pope John XXIII, Julian of Norwich, and Mary Magdalene in the church's pantheon.

One of the saints of St. Gregory's is the Trappist monk and author Thomas Merton. His presence in the lineup reminds me of someone I think Merton himself would nominate for sainthood—and I'd second the motion. I'm thinking of Mark Van Doren, the Pulitzer Prize–winning poet and author who influenced so many students during his long and distinguished tenure as professor of English at Columbia University. In his spiritual classic *The Seven Storey Mountain,* Merton credits Van Doren for keeping him from falling under the sway of campus Communism, and preparing him for his vocation as a priest, because of "the influence of Mark's sober and sincere intellect, and his manner of dealing with his subject with perfect honesty and objectivity and without evasion." Van Doren possessed what Merton called "a kind of heroic humility," that "honors his profession and makes it fruitful." Merton, the grateful student, believed that this professor was "no stranger to the order of grace," and that "Providence was using him as an instrument more directly than he realized."

Van Doren influenced succeeding generations with his generosity of spirit as well as his literary insights. A decade after Merton was there, a young poet named Allen Ginsberg rushed into the office of the Columbia English Department and shouted excitedly, "I have just seen the light!" The other professors who were present nervously cleared their throats and muttered that they had to hurry to a class. Van Doren stayed, and asked the young poet, "What was it like?" It may have been that incident that led Allen Ginsberg to comment later that the rest of the professors in the Columbia English Department were interested in "careers in literature," while Van Doren was interested in "illuminated wisdom."

A friend of Ginsberg's who played on the Columbia football team was so moved by Van Doren's Shakespeare course that he quit the team to devote more time to writing. His name was Jack Kerouac, and Van Doren recommended his first novel *(The Town and the City)* to another former student, the editor Robert Giroux, who published it at Farrar, Straus. Ginsberg once told me, "At Columbia I found nourishment from Van Doren—spiritual nourishment. He had a spiritual gift."

I was lucky enough to find that gift myself when I went to Columbia, inspired by an essay of Van Doren's, and took his courses in poetry and the narrative art. He taught us that the great lesson of *Don Quixote* was that "the way to become a knight is to act like a knight—do the things a knight does." He believed the same principle applied to saints. Merton ran into Van Doren on the street once and told him a friend of his had said something that struck him as impossible, if not ludicrous: "All a person needs to be a saint is to want to be one."

Van Doren said, "Of course."

Newsweek called Van Doren a "living legend"; now that he is gone I propose we call him a saint.

Who do you think should be a saint? And why?

20

Can a Greenwich Village Radical Become a Saint?: Dorothy Day

Will the Roman Catholic Church confer sainthood on a Greenwich Village radical and activist who had an abortion, was divorced, and bore a lover's child out of wedlock?

Surprising as it seems, Dorothy Day, the controversial founder of the Catholic Worker movement, antiwar demonstrator, and outspoken opponent of Senator Joe McCarthy in his heyday, has been approved for the process of study that leads to canonization in the Church, twenty years after her death.

It seems to me that Dorothy Day illustrates one of the key ingredients of sainthood: not only did she do good for others, she inspired others to do good. Her influence was not just a positive factor in helping people better their own lives, but led them to work for the betterment of the lives of others. Another element that seems to be part of genuine sainthood is that the influence of such people is not limited to their own time and place, but seems to go out in waves, like light, not only to different places, but to different times.

I first met Dorothy Day right after I graduated from Columbia and was living in Greenwich Village. That fall of 1955 I published my first magazine article in *The Nation,* and a college friend took me to see the Catholic Worker Hospitality House in the Bowery as a subject to write about. I was fascinated by the mix of recently revived winos and idealistic young intellectuals drawn there by the vision of this Catholic convert who was living her Christianity in service to the poor. At the other mission houses in the Bowery, you had to "sing for your supper" by claiming you were saved and joining in a hymn, but at the Catholic Worker you only needed to be hungry.

I was awed by Dorothy herself, a woman Michael Harrington described in his memoir *Fragments of the Century* as severe yet serene, like "a mystic out of a Dostoevsky novel." Her gray hair was done in a braid pinned up in the back; she wore no makeup, stood ramrod straight, and commanded a room by her very presence. When psychiatrist/author Robert Coles was in medical school at Columbia, he went to the Bowery to meet her, only to find her engrossed in a conversation with a drunken woman. After a while Dorothy looked up and asked Coles, "Are you waiting to talk with one of us?" Dr. Coles knew at once what her priorities were, and he became a volunteer, later a friend, and wrote about her in *Dorothy Day: A Radical Devotion.*

The article I wrote about the Catholic Worker in *The Nation* was called "Miracle in the Bowery," and after it was published, Dorothy didn't speak to me. I learned that she objected to my quoting from Malcolm Cowley's book *Exiles*

Return that Dorothy had been one of the few who could drink Eugene O'Neill under the table. I thought it was a noble claim to fame; Dorothy thought it was a glamorization of the 1920s mythology of booze as the muse, a destructive message she didn't want to pass on.

Dorothy's message was one of selfless service, and her example of it inspired young people from across the country in the buttoned-down Eisenhower Age—the age of *The Organization Man* and *How to Succeed in Business*—to seek a different, more meaningful life. As a young intellectual from St. Louis, Michael Harrington came to live and work at the Catholic Worker House on Chrystie Street for two years, finding the understanding that later led to his book *The Other America,* which inspired Lyndon Johnson's poverty program.

A novice nun named Helen Russell in a convent in California was discovered playing Ravel's *Bolero* and the Mother Superior told her, "I know where you belong," and handed her a copy of the penny newspaper of the Catholic Worker. Helen got on a bus to New York and went to the Hospitality House in the Bowery, later teaming up with two other young women she met there to move to East Harlem and open a day care center for children. I met these young women when I wrote my article, went to East Harlem to see their work, and moved to the neighborhood to write my first book, *Island in the City: The World of Spanish Harlem.*

The poet Ned O'Gorman went down from college in Vermont to volunteer at the Catholic Worker in 1954, and I interviewed him in the 1990s when he was running the Storefront School for Children in Harlem, which he founded.

He told me, "I sometimes think I'm here in some way because I soaked up Dorothy's vision of the human family. Her influence was profound." Mike Harrington said he was "one of hundreds of thousands who were influenced by her life."

That influence continues, multiplies, lights up new lives with hope and inspiration, shines like a nimbus—"a radiant light that appears in the form of a circle or halo about or over the head of a god, saint, or sacred person."

21

A Monk in Love:
Thomas Merton

Like countless people around the world, I have long regarded the Trappist monk Thomas Merton, author of the classic spiritual autobiography *The Seven Storey Mountain,* as an icon of contemporary spirituality, a modern saint. He lived at the monastery of Gethsemani in the hills of Kentucky and in later years, for deeper contemplation, moved from the main house to a single-room dwelling called the Hermitage.

Merton not only wrote an autobiography that became a worldwide best-seller but also dozens of other books and hundreds of articles, inspiring not only Christians but followers of many faiths. In his later years he began a dialogue with leaders of Eastern religions and traveled to Buddhist conferences in Asia, dying in a freak accident in Bangkok in 1968 at age fifty-three.

Although Bishop Fulton J. Sheen praised *The Seven Storey Mountain* on its publication in 1948 as "a twentieth-century form of *The Confessions of St. Augustine,*" it turns out that Merton saved his deepest confessions for the private journals he kept over a period of twenty-nine years, and restricted from publication until twenty-five years after his death. Published in seven volumes, the last released in 1998, these confessions reveal what Merton's own admirers regard as spiritual "scandals."

A perceptive evaluation of the entire work by Jonathan Montaldo, former director of the Thomas Merton Center at Bellarmine College in Louisville, warns in an article on Merton's spirituality ("Loving Winter When the Plant Says Nothing") that these volumes of personal history will "scandalize the reader who seeks in them a spiritual success story to emulate."

Torn between earthly love and priestly vows, Merton confides that he became in his early fifties "a priest who has a woman." The woman was a young nurse whom he met and fell in love with during a stay in a Louisville hospital, and arranged to see after he returned to the monastery. This was during the time he was living in supposed isolation at the Hermitage on the grounds of Gethsemani in what was assumed to be a state of the highest sort of purity and piety, and writing books and essays that his many followers looked to for spiritual guidance (and still do today).

In his journals of this period (1966–68), Merton writes that he was saddened to find himself reverting to the behavior of his rebellious youth in Greenwich Village. With opportunities to leave the community for travel to spiritual conferences around the world and visits to the hospital in Louisville, he found himself acting "wild." He was drinking, as he had in his youth, and friends were sending him "care packages" that included gourmet food and bottles of Jack Daniels.

Here I was imagining this supposed giant of self-discipline dozing off in his hermitage after a night of prayer and fasting, when actually he was knocking back a couple of shots of Jack Daniels (Black Label, no doubt, the best) and dreaming of the next rendezvous with his nubile nurse! I felt I'd been hoodwinked. The more I read about these revelations and Merton's struggles with them, however, the less judgmental I became of his failures and the more appreciative of his willingness to lay bare his soul.

Montaldo, who began a lifelong study of Merton when he read him at age thirteen, points out that the monk in his confessions "places before the eyes of his readers their own struggle with conflicting desires which attend their own spiritual journeying." Merton made the point in a later preface to his first book that "it is not as an author that I would speak to you, not as a storyteller, not as a philosopher, not as a friend only: I seek to speak to you, in some way, as your own self."

That message spoke to me, for in Merton's record of his wrestling match with God, I can see my own continuing struggles to discern—much less follow—a spiritual path.

As Merton wrestled with his own conflicting desires after falling in love at age fifty-one, he wrote, "I am thrown into contradiction: to realize it is mercy, to accept it is love, to help others do the same is compassion." This is the kind of message of self-forgiveness conveyed in the works of Thomas Moore like *Care of the Soul,* which a wide audience, including me, is glad to hear.

Merton ended the relationship with the nurse, but his struggles with trying to live by his ideals continued. To ask why he withheld these journals until twenty-five years after his death may be answered in part by realizing the vast change in our culture's acceptance of personal confessions that became not only acceptable but fashionable in the 1990s. In the past decade Americans have outdone one another in scandalous revelations, from an author's adult sex with her father to an academic's boyhood sex with his dog. The axiom now is "The worse you've behaved, the better your sales." A fifty-one-year-old monk sneaking out from the monastery to rendezvous with a young nurse would today land him on *Oprah* and the best-seller list.

Though Merton never had to face that particular temptation, he acknowledged his own desire for public acclaim, warning himself that "fame is the beginning of disgrace." Part of him wanted to be "a pontiff, prophet, and writer" but he felt he needed to renounce all that to be the contemplative monk he set out to be. The pull between ego-gratifying public praise and selfless service to God was a struggle that never ended, another one that many of us can identify with but few of us have the courage—and the grace—to acknowledge.

I am grateful to Merton now for his confessions, including what must have been the most difficult thing of all for a Roman Catholic monk and world-renowned spiritual leader to reveal: that even the most complete commitment to God does not guarantee peace or happiness or human fulfillment, but may indeed lead to interior conflict, struggle, and anguish. The greatest gift of Merton's private journals is to show us that even our gurus go through the darkness in seeking the light, and in our spiritual failures we are not alone.

22

The Spiritual Legacy of a Pagan: C. Wright Mills

"The average ministerial output is correctly heard as a parade of outworn phrases. It is generally unimaginative and often trivial. As public rhetoric, it is boring and irrelevant. As private belief, it is without passion."

Those words might have been written today by a number of critics of mainline religion, including some faithful Christian and Jewish believers. That critique, however, was spoken nearly half a century ago to a conclave of Protestant clergy by a leading social critic who was invited to address them on "Religion and War, or Moral Insensibility" in the heyday of the Cold War. The evangelical board of the United Churches of Canada may have got more than they bargained for when they invited as their speaker C. Wright Mills, the maverick sociologist whose books like *White Collar* and *The Power Elite* shook up the complacency of the 1950s, and served as inspiration for the student radicals of the 1960s.

Mills called his talk to the ministers "A Pagan Sermon to the Christian Clergy," and it became the basis for another of his controversial books, *The Causes of World War III*. At a time when the United States and the Soviet Union were engaged in a nuclear arms race that threatened to blow up not only each other but the whole world, Mills was calling on Christian ministers to speak out against the madness, "to serve as a moral conscience and to articulate that conscience." Mills followed the Quaker dictum to "speak truth to power," and while he admired the ministers' nonviolent protests against the arms race and their willingness to take political stands, he did not join them or any other religious group, any more than he joined any political party or movement, preferring to "go it alone."

A visitor who couldn't fit him into a political pigeonhole asked once, "What do you believe in, Mills?" At the moment Mills was tinkering with his beloved BMW motorcycle (he rode it from his home in Nyack, New York, to his office at Columbia on 116th and Broadway) and he answered without hesitation: "German motors." In his "pagan sermon" to the clergy, Mills said that, according to their belief, he was "among the damned," for he was "secular, prideful, agnostic, and all the rest of it."

He was also, I believe, a spiritual man, in the broadest and deepest sense of the term. The aim of Mills's "sermon," and the book that was born from it, was a plea for life in a literal way, an argument against the death of the human race and the planet through a nuclear holocaust that was being debated in the Cold War era as a rational outcome of political policy. The thrust of all his work was toward the fullness of life, the goal of what he called "taking it big" in all aspects of experience, from work to play, and against the influence of the "cheerful robots" of white collar conformity and the "crackpot realists" of political expedience.

I knew Mills first as a professor, when I took a seminar he gave at Columbia, then later as an employer, when I served as his research assistant for a book he was working on, and, finally, as a friend, until his untimely death in 1962 at the age of forty-five. I recently renewed and deepened my appreciation of Mills and his work when I wrote the introduction to a book of his letters (C. *Wright Mills: Letters and Autobiographical Writings,* edited by Kathryn Mills, with Pamela Mills). The letters, personal and vulnerable, are the eloquent testimony of a seeker, whose spirituality emerges not in religious terms, but in care for his friends and fellow human beings, in the passion for learning and perfecting one's craft, for enjoying and appreciating the commonplace gifts of everyday experience, and finding in them the inspiration for living more fully.

A fellow intellectual friend who was depressed wrote to Mills asking him what there was to get excited about in life anymore, and this was Mills's answer:

"You ask for what one should be keyed up? My god, for long weekends in the country, and snow and the feel of an idea and New York streets early in the morning and late at night and the camera eye always working whether you want it to or not and yes by god how the earth feels when it's been plowed deep and the new chartreuse wall in the study and wine before dinner and if you can afford it Irish whiskey afterwards and sawdust in your pants cuff and sometimes at evening the dusky pink sky to the northwest, and books to read never touched and all that stuff the Greeks wrote and have you ever read Macauley's speeches to hear the English language? And to revise your mode of talk and what you talk about and yes by god the world of music which we just now discover and there's still hot jazz and getting a car out of the mud when nobody else can. That's what the hell to get keyed up about."

In his letters as in his books, this "pagan" agnostic left us a true sense of spirit, as defined in the *Oxford English Dictionary*: "The animating or vital principle in humans (and animals); that which gives life; the breath of life."

23

We Have the Power to Change: Werner Erhard

"At all times, under all circumstances, we have the power to transform the quality of our lives." That was the message Werner Erhard brought with his weekend seminars that launched the movements of personal growth and human potential to a nationwide audience in the 1970s. Erhard's "technology of transformation" drew more than a million people to his est training, and its current outgrowth, the Forum. His work has earned him the respect and gratitude of supporters—some of whom have compared him to a saint—and the enmity and outrage of critics, who have called him everything from a "pop guru" to "a monster of selfishness."

Erhard disclaims both extremes of saint and monster; he told a group of Irish priests and nuns at a workshop he led in Dublin in the 1990s: "In Zen they say there's a high road to enlightenment and a low road. I took the low road. On the low road, you do everything that doesn't work."

After *60 Minutes* aired an all-out attack on Erhard in 1991, he left the United States, and continued his work in Europe and Asia. It was widely reported in the press that he was fleeing the country to evade back taxes, but only one

American newspaper (the *Los Angeles Daily News*) published the story when he later was vindicated with a $200,000 settlement from the IRS. In a rare positive press account, *Time* magazine reported in 1998 that the key charges of the *60 Minutes* attack on Erhard had been disproved or recanted.

Erhard believes that the negative press began because of the novelty of his program when it was launched in 1971. "There was no model for it," he told me. "If it got people to change, people thought it must be a 'religion,' and if it was, it shouldn't be making money. There were a lot of misconceptions and misunderstandings in the beginning because it was new and there was no category for it."

Drawing an analogy between his work and religion, *Newsweek* once suggested that "Erhard has captured the imagination of the upper-middle classes much as Billy Graham has collared the humbler masses."

Just as many people feared that yoga would cause participants to leave their own religion, so many feared the same of a seminar promising "transformation." Ironically, some of the major religious leaders in the United States believed that Erhard's program could only empower their own work as ministers, priests, and rabbis, and went to him for help in creating a program designed specially for them and their professional colleagues.

Father M. Basil Pennington, the Trappist monk and author of the influential book *Centering Prayer,* was so impressed by the est training that in 1983 he joined with other clergy who wanted to bring the technology of transformation to people in religious life, and formed the

Mastery Foundation. Pennington was joined in this effort by other noted clergy, including Bishop Otis Charles, dean of the Episcopal Divinity School in Cambridge, Massachusetts, until his retirement in 1994. With Erhard's assistance they designed a program that combined his technology of transformation with Pennington's centering prayer, and called it Making a Difference in Ministry. Erhard contributed his own work, but purposely stayed out of the Mastery Foundation, fearing that his presence in a program designed for religious leaders would stir too much controversy.

Father Pennington told me he did Erhard's work after meeting an MIT student who read his book *Centering Prayer* and started a group to practice it. Pennington learned that "she had left her home and religion at age twelve, but two years previous to our meeting she did the est training, and it opened up her life. She reconciled with her family and her church, and decided to become a Trappist nun. I'd never heard of est—in a monastery you miss a lot—but five weeks later I went to hear Werner Erhard talk about his Hunger Project.

"I was impressed by his approach, and he asked me to be on the advisory board of the Hunger Project, which I agreed to if I could see everything they did, and he said okay. I did est as Werner's guest, and heard about the Center for Contextual Study, which came out of his work to help therapists gain mastery in their profession. It was extremely effective, and I thought 'Why don't we capture this approach for ministry?'"

Bishop Charles told me, "The two individuals most influential in shaping my manner of grappling with work and life in the last fifteen years are Werner Erhard and St.

Ignatius of Loyola. The two are separated by about four hundred years, but each had a gift of being able to put together a way of creating a space in which your own life and gifts were able to be clearly manifested."

Father Pennington and Erhard together led the first Mastery of Ministry workshop in Massachusetts in 1984, creating the course as they went along. "We agreed he'd stay out of the 'God talk,' and there'd be no theology," Pennington explained, because the program was meant for men and women of all religious backgrounds. "I taught Werner centering prayer, and he saw that as fulfillment of what he was aiming at—being at peace with yourself and at one with God." *Centering prayer* is a modern term for the contemplative practice begun in the second or third century in the Christian tradition, a form that novice monks learned as "the prayer of the heart."

I asked Father Pennington how he felt Erhard's work related to ministry.

"When Pope Paul VI asked us to help the church reform the contemplative dimension in 1972, I found the hardest people to reach were the clergy—they're so stuck in their heads after years of theology. I thought Werner's work was a way of getting people out of their heads and into reality. A very high percentage of those who have done our workshop feel it helped their ministry and personal life. We've had to work against a lot of prejudices—prejudice against the contemplative dimension, and against the ecumenical nature of our work. I'm proud we provide a good ecumenical experience—people come who have prejudice against one religion or other and get completely free of it—it's beautiful to see."

When Erhard led the workshop for priests and nuns in Dublin, he began with the same sort of qualified invitation he uses for all his programs: "You've all been listening to me for a half hour or so," he says. "And to some of you what I've been saying may have struck a chord; it may 'call to you.' If that's the case, you should do this program. For others, what I've said simply may not 'call to you,' and if that's the case, you shouldn't do it."

Sharply dressed in a gray tweed jacket, gray slacks, and a black shirt buttoned at the neck without a tie, Erhard spoke in his firm, stare-you-down style, expressing deep respect for his audience: "For me," he told them, "people who choose to use their lives as priests or nuns are special. I respect the courage it takes to make a religious commitment—it's not the easy road to travel.

"I'm privately very religious, since I was small," he said. "I sit in church and tears roll down my eyes—but it's personal. I don't have expertise, I'm not a theologian. I'm going to find out what ministry is through *you*."

After many definitions were offered, Erhard said, "There's no such thing as ministry, it only arises in language—it's not fixed, so you can't 'get it right'—it's generative, so you are free to create, invent, constitute, generate your ministry…. You can create it as something ennobling, empowering." As in other seminars he conducts, Erhard urged the participants to "try on, like a jacket" his ideas, rather than "believe" them, to see things in a new context, and "take with you only what fits, which means it came from you, not me, anyway."

In his controversial method of challenge, Erhard questioned, provoked, and even yelled at the priests and nuns. "I try to treat people with ruthless compassion because I don't see them as frail or weak," he told them. "I have no love for suffering and don't want to elevate it to any glory. If you want to be 'heartfelt' about something, be heartfelt about something meaningful, like the opportunity of your ministry—not the difficulties you suffered in life."

He stopped, pointed at his audience accusingly and shouted: "You're *church mice* about your ministry—and powerfully expressive about the terrible things that have happened to you! It's fine for the Irish poets and playwrights to celebrate the misery life can hold—the rest of you, *cut it out!*"

He treated them as he does others in his seminars, which not only meant confronting, but also praising with equal zeal. "Don, thank you for sharing, I mean *really,* it took a big person to do that.... Liz, you're a beautiful, powerful woman—use your power!"

At a break, Father Frankie Murray said, "For someone they call a guru, Werner's not bad—he's an okay guy. The Irish don't go for gurus—I'd have been uncomfortable with that. He's not trying to empower people to be what they're not—but to be who they are."

24

Communicating with the Unseen: Ollah Toph

I've never seen angels with halos or wings, but I've known flesh-and-blood people I felt were guardian angels in my life, and whose presence I have sensed after their death. First and foremost I think of "Aunt Ollie," who opened me up to such possibilities—to the reality and beneficence of the unseen—when I was a fourteen-year-old boy in Indianapolis.

Her name was Ollah Toph and she was not really my aunt but a distant cousin on my mother's side of the family. She was famous among my relatives—or infamous, depending on your viewpoint—for being able to foretell the future, as she did one summer afternoon when she called my grandmother to ask "Where is Charles?" He was my mother's younger brother, the favorite son of my grandma Irene (known as "Ireney"), and she reported that this bright twenty-one-year-old was on vacation at a lake in Michigan and wondered why Aunt Ollie wanted to know. The chilling reply, carved in our family's history, was: "I sense death and water." Charles drowned that afternoon.

My parents took me to Aunt Ollie when I was beginning to suffer the angst of adolescence, hoping perhaps that this woman in her eighties could bring some kind of hope or comfort to a troubled teenage boy. She lived north of town in a house that was like a cabin in the woods, filled with books that included a privately printed volume of her spiritual poems that were published in local newspapers, and a foot-pedal organ she played with love. With a beautiful crown of snow-white hair, Ollah Toph was a striking woman of great poise and dignity.

As well as being an organist and poet, Aunt Ollie was a clairvoyant, and a dedicated member of the Spiritualist Church, which she had served as a delegate to a conference in England attended by Arthur Conan Doyle (a yellowed clipping in her scrapbook testified to the event). She believed that when people died, their souls or spirits went to a higher plane, and that some of them looked over us in that role we call "guardian angel." She believed she sometimes could communicate with those souls, which was part of her religion, along with her belief in God and Christ, which she conveyed in a sensitive manner in some of her verse. She was offended by any suggestion of being a "fortune teller" or dabbler in the occult. The spirit, and the spirits, were simply part of her life and its meaning.

To ask her to use her powers of seeing or communicating beyond the five senses would have insulted her, but if she were in the appropriate mood she would sometimes close her eyes, and with a sharp intake of breath, describe a person standing beside us whom we could not see, yet we sensed as she spoke, perhaps saying, "Danny, I see a tall man standing beside you, wearing a vest and a gold watch chain across it..." By a sign or gesture from the "presence" that only

Aunt Ollie herself could see, a sense of interest and protection was conveyed, an aura of benevolence.

There were also times when Aunt Ollie would take my hand or the hand of my mother or father, and in a deep, trancelike state that seemed sacred, speak of the future. On one occasion I still remember clearly, she took my hand and said "Danny, you will be close to death through some experience that will interrupt your education, but you will survive it, and complete your education. Then you will cross several oceans—the Atlantic, and oceans beyond it—to a farther land than Europe."

In Indianapolis in the 1940s, that seemed as remote as something out of the Arabian Nights. The remembrance of it came as a comfort when I had to leave college for a semester after suffering a broken and dislocated cervical vertebra in an automobile wreck that could have killed me or left me paralyzed after my junior year in college. I missed a semester, graduated from Columbia the following February, and the following January of 1956 went to Israel to write a series of articles for *The Nation* magazine. As I was standing on the deck of the SS *Israel,* approaching Haifa, Aunt Ollie's words came back to me. The memory of what she had said at first brought a chill, and then a warming sense that there is a power in the universe beyond what we can touch or see, that our lives are part of a more profound mystery than we can hope to understand. That mystery, for me, leads to God.

25

Clear Vision:
Reynolds Price

When a large cancer was discovered in novelist Reynolds Price's spinal cord, he was given no hope of recovery. "The tumor was pencil-thick and gray-colored, 10 inches long from my neck-hair down," he wrote in *A Whole New Life: An Illness and a Healing,* his nonfiction account of the experience. Radical surgeries, radiation, severe pain, and reliance on drugs rendered him paraplegic and consigned him to a wheelchair—yet those dire circumstances ended neither his life nor his brilliant career. A writer whose fiction has gone against contemporary literary fashion by making God and religion a natural part of his characters' lives, Price called upon his own lifelong faith in God and his dedication as an artist to sustain him.

Rather than being defeated by his devastating illness, the author used it as an occasion for becoming more prolific, declaring that the confinement it brought gave him more time and opportunity to focus: "In 10 years since the tumor was found, I've completed 13 books—I'd published a first 12 in the previous 22 years," he wrote in *A Whole New Life,* adding that "panic came elsewhere but never in my work." Instead of destroying his faith, the disaster deepened his spiritual life, bringing a healing vision of Jesus that gave him hope through the worst of the suffering. He found relief from pain through the alternative medical practices of biofeedback and hypnosis after prescribed drugs had brought only grogginess and despair. Mining art out of illness, he transformed early childhood memories that surfaced in hypnotic healing sessions and led to a memoir of childhood called *Clear Pictures.*

When the illness struck him at age fifty-one, Price was at work on the novel *Kate Vaiden,* which he completed during his painful struggle for survival; it won the National Book Critics Circle Award in 1986. The prize highlighted a career that began when Price burst onto the literary scene at age twenty-nine with his debut novel, *A Long and Happy Life,* which was initially published in its entirety in a single issue of *Harper's* magazine in 1962, went on to win the William Faulkner Award for a notable first novel, and has never been out of print since. A former Rhodes scholar from a small town in North Carolina, Price has taught every spring semester since 1958 at Duke University, his alma mater.

Inspired by the depth of his passion and understanding—and his rare example of an American literary figure of my time who wrote with conviction of being a Christian—I began to reread Price's books and to look forward to new ones. I welcomed the opportunity to talk with him about his work.

DW: *You say that the first "ground-level question" you asked God when you learned of your illness was not "Why me?" but "What's next?" That's an unusual response. Did you have any uncommon reactions to other aspects of your ordeal?*

RP: I was surprised to find out how many of my doctors, nurses, and counselors were always saying to me, "Get your anger out." I couldn't think of anything to be angry at. I couldn't be angry at cancer. I couldn't be angry at my legs for refusing to work. There's a whole level of rage in this country that is supposed to be so healthy for us: "Get it out—let's all go scream for two hours." No.

DW: *When you were stricken with the illness, were there any helpful models of writers or artists who survived such ordeals?*

RP: Music was crucial to me. When he first heard I was sick, [English poet] Stephen Spender bought me a Sony Walkman, which I had barely heard of before. I listened to thousands of hours of music, and occasionally I would recall that Bach and Handel had gone blind and Beethoven deaf. When you're in that boat, you certainly collect fellows in misery. And, of course, I thought a lot about Flannery O'Connor, who didn't make it out of her ordeal [of lupus], though she wrote magnificently while she was in the ordeal. Those were definitely important figures for me.

DW: *In* Three Gospels, *you go against current theological fashion. You uphold the literal truth of much of the New Testament, while the Jesus Seminar [a group of scholars working to determine the historical facts of Jesus' life] seems to be trying to disprove the miracles and healings of Jesus, as well as his own words.*

RP: I have many reasons for feeling that the Jesus Seminar has been more flash than substance. I've read a lot of their publications, and some have been very interesting and useful. I don't think they're charlatans or people who have set out to overturn anything. But it really is sort of touching and amusing to see them trying to apply scientific method to human history—or take the hopeless stand that if you can't prove that Jesus said so-and-so, then he didn't say it. How are you going to prove what was said two thousand years ago?

DW: I once interviewed John Dominic Crossan, one of the theologians of the Jesus Seminar, and I asked if he had read your essay on John 21 [the story of Jesus appearing to the disciples after the crucifixion as they are fishing on the Sea of Galilee], which, you argue as a writer, seems like a literal account of an actual occurrence. Father Crossan had not read your essay, and when I told him that I agreed with you about the literal reality of the story, he said, "I think you've both been taken in by a good novelist."

RP: I think it's the most wonderful story in the world, and it still is to me—I don't care what Crossan or anyone else thinks. It has a ring of reality that doesn't sound like fiction writing to me. If it is fiction writing, then whoever John was invented the techniques of the modern novel single-handedly, overnight, in the first century!

DW: You've discussed a concept of literature I haven't heard for a long time—literature as a way of teaching people how to live.

RP: It's one of the aspects of literature that's been greatly ignored. It's how the ancients used Homer—they used him as a model of how to be a virtuous man and a great warrior, and how to treat the gods. I think it's easy to lose that, and to a great extent we've lost it. It's why we have so many how-to books.

DW: *You're a devoted Christian, but you don't go to church. Is it true that that's because of your disillusionment with Protestant churches in the South during the civil rights movement?*

RP: The real point at which I simply ceased going to church on any regular basis was when I lived in England on the Rhodes scholarship—just being a young man in a foreign country deciding I wasn't going to get up on Sunday. By the time I got back to America, I'd gotten out of the habit, and also at that time the civil rights movement was cranking up full blast, and, as everybody knows, the Southern, white Christian church behaved about as badly as possible.

The few times I've gone to church in recent years, I'm immediately asked if I'll coach the Little League team or give a talk on Wednesday night or come to the men's bell-ringing class on Sunday afternoon. Church has become a full-service entertainment facility. It ought to be the place where God lives.

DW: *You wrote that you spend a good deal of your week "in prayer or in other kinds of activity which I know are distinctly religious or distinctively identifiable as negotiations with the supernatural, and I don't feel the need for conducting them in the presence of others." What are your daily rituals?*

RP: Ninety-nine percent of it is internal experience—a sentence said in prayer here and there, or a thought. I guess I sort of do it all day long as I am working.

DW: *Your work has been about love in all of its manifestations, including sexual, but without the sense of guilt that I find in many Christian writers.*

RP: It does seem that someone who has grown up in a Christian church atmosphere is very likely to come up with a sense of guilt about sexuality. I think I got a minimum of those messages largely because my parents were extremely decent people and thought of themselves as Christians, though they weren't totally "churchy." They went to church, but it wasn't an obsession, and they seemed to have a wonderful sex life. I obviously didn't witness it, but I witnessed the results of it in their great tenderness for each other.

All my life, sex has remained important, though obviously paraplegia seriously revises anyone's relationship to his or her body sexually. I feel sadness when I run across people who can't enjoy their sexuality. It has been for me a source of reward.

DW: *Your novel* The Promise of Rest *talks about every kind of sexuality in a more honest, enlightening way than any novel I know, yet you've never written or talked publicly about your own sexuality.*

RP: I think it's partly a generational thing. You and I came from a world where the individual private life was just not the subject of conversation. It's always seemed to me that if your sex life can't be private, what can? I'm not at all interested in lying to anyone or deceiving anyone, and I've never tried to do that. It's just that I've always resisted answering the specific, individual questions of who's who in your own life and what's what.

DW: *Somebody told me you gave a talk once and a man in the audience asked point-blank, "Are you a homosexual?" and you said, "Why—do you find me attractive?"*

RP: No, I said, "Have you suddenly fallen in love with me?" He fled the room! It was one of those moments of inspiration that come all too rarely—something you usually think of in bed the next night. But he really was terribly flummoxed by it.

DW: *In addition to being a successful and prolific writer, you teach a writing course every year, and some of your students have gone on to be successful writers themselves, such as Anne Tyler. Do you have any advice on writing?*

RP: It took me forever to realize that in order to write I just have to turn up at the desk every morning at 9:00 A.M. and do it. I usually try to take Sunday off. I don't say, "I don't feel up to it today." Unless I have a doctor's appointment, I have to be at my desk. And I can never convince kids of this. Faulkner said something wonderful about it when somebody asked him, "Mr. Faulkner, do you write by inspiration or perspiration?" He said, "Well, I write by inspiration, but fortunately it arrives every morning at nine o'clock."

26

Be Old Now:
Ram Dass

When I heard that Ram Dass, author of the 1960s spiritual manifesto *Be Here Now,* was leading a weekend workshop on Conscious Aging in Clearwater, Florida, I signed up right away. I was just getting used to being an "old guy"—a term I find more direct and less condescending than "senior citizen"—and I was anxious to hear about any new ways of understanding the subject. Who better to provide a fresh insight on age than Ram Dass, the popular guru of the Woodstock generation—the generation that made youth a cult.

In his previous incarnation as Harvard professor Richard Alpert, Ram Dass teamed with Timothy Leary to turn on undergraduates with psilocybin and spread the word of illumination-through-hallucination to the flower children. Bounced out of Harvard, Alpert looked East to find enlightenment with a guru in India, shedding tweeds and loafers for a robe and sandals, and trading in his birth name for a Sanskrit moniker meaning "servant of God." Though we have traveled far different paths, Ram Dass and I are the same age, and I knew that his outlook on growing old wouldn't be burdened by conformity to prevailing "gerontology," defined by *Webster* as "the study of the physiological and pathological phenomena associated with aging." (This is not just a stage of life, it's a "pathology"!)

More than two hundred of us over-sixties, mixed with younger people who make a living by studying, caring for, nursing, or selling housing to "elders," gathered in the Tiffany Ballroom of the Belleview Mido Resort Hotel in Clearwater, Florida, for the third annual conference on Conscious Aging sponsored by the Omega Institute. It was 1995, and the subject was just getting hot. "You know when you've really hit on something," an Omega program director said. Aging was the big new drawing card on the self-help circuit, and of course it made sense—the baby boomers were now passing fifty, so it figured that aging had become a "movement."

Ram Dass appeared before us in a red-and-white shirt hanging loose over khaki pants, and brown moccasins without socks. The top of his head was bald, and red from the sun, with white hair flowing out from the sides like foam. Some of his fans hadn't seen him since they sat at his feet with hundreds of others to hear the wisdom he brought back from India in the 1970s, and they were shocked at the signs of his own aging. "He's gray," said one, while another, more surprised, gasped, "He's fat!" Ram Dass later that day looked down at his stomach and described it as a "guru belly."

Ram Dass settled down on a wicker couch on a platform overlooking our rows of hotel chairs. Some zealous elder had stuck a red-and-white bumper sticker on the couch that read "Sexy Senior Citizen." Ram Dass plucked it off and said, "As an antidote to this, I'll tell you a story.

"An older man is walking down the street one day when a frog jumps up on his arm and says, 'If you kiss me, I'll turn into a beautiful princess and do whatever you want.' The man sticks the frog in his pocket and walks on. After a few more blocks the frog croaks, 'Hey, don't you want to kiss me so I'll turn into your beautiful princess?' The man says, 'At this stage of life, I'd rather have a talking frog.'"

This got a rousing laugh from the audience, which didn't seem to bode well for overcoming the "mythology of aging."

Ram Dass pulled a few Perrier bottles from a black knapsack, set them on a table with a photograph of his guru, and told us he'd come to this subject through a sudden awareness of his own aging. A year or so earlier on a train from Westport, Connecticut, to New York City, a conductor had asked him what kind of ticket he wanted—senior citizen or regular.

"I was pleased to learn I could buy a 'senior' ticket at half the fare," Ram Dass remembered, "but I wondered how in the world the conductor knew I was a 'senior citizen.' He didn't even ask for my ID. I realized then, *I am a senior citizen.* I had never put those words together—'I' and 'senior citizen.' It blew my mind. I thought, 'What does it feel like to be a senior citizen?' and immediately I felt myself contracting, bent over—I started feeling how society defines me as old. Being a senior citizen is not necessarily a bargain. Our society is so youth-oriented it treats older people as 'less than.'

"A few years ago in an Indian village I met a brother devotee of my guru and he said, 'You're looking much older.' I drew back, offended, then I saw he was saying it with respect, not diminishment, like it was an accomplishment.

My reaction showed how I'd bought into my culture's attitude, and I realized I'd have to be mindful. I remembered that when you put frogs in hot water they jump out, but if you put them in cold water and slowly heat it, they sit there and boil to death. I realized, 'Unless I am mindful, I'll boil to death'—I'll slide into the model of aging in my culture and lose power, social role, economic and political power. I was awed by the dysfunctional mythology about aging in our society."

Ram Dass said we needed "a new mythology of aging."

"In gerontology," he told us, "aging seems to be presented as a problem, as something with suffering inherent—in loss, grief, fear of death. My speculation is that it's possible to bring inner practice to bear on the phenomenon we call aging, so it's not overwhelming and doesn't contract or define us."

As he spoke, Ram Dass fingered a string of beads.

"When you're young, you rehearse the future, when you're old you rehearse the past, but you're never in the present moment! We need a shift in perspective, to acknowledge a different identity. In India death is 'dropping the body.' Our philosophically material society says, 'I am body, mind, and senses,' so when that goes, you're gone.

"There's a way of looking at your life from a different vantage point. Only through identity as a soul can you go without suffering."

Ram Dass's approach to conscious aging seemed the same as it was for any other stage of life, as expressed in his popular books and lectures like *Be Here Now, The Only Dance There Is,* and *Grist for the Mill.* He teaches people why and how to be in the moment, through meditation, "witnessing" of the self, and trying to consciously separate from the ego that runs our lives.

After Ram Dass finished his talk, he said his good-byes, which turned out to be a half-hour "hugathon." More than thirty people lined up to get a hug, and he gave each one his full attention and a wholehearted embrace. I'd arranged to interview Ram Dass after the session, and as we walked to his hotel suite he told me, "Hugging is a very high form of transmission. To hug without desire is an art form. If somebody comes up and presses their pelvic bones against you, you just wait. You wait, and then it's okay."

He made a few phone calls from his suite, offered me chocolates from a box someone gave him, pulled up a chair, and stretched his legs out to rest on a couch. I asked if people pressing their pelvic bones against him was part of the temptation of being a guru and asked how he handled it.

"Sometimes people come up to me who I'm attracted to and want to have sex, but I can't afford the karma," he said. "I tell them 'I'd love to, but I don't think we can afford it.'"

Lovemaking is "appropriate in old age" if it is "a form of communion that is less impulse-driven," according to Rabbi Zalman Schachter-Shalomi, who Ram Dass said is the pioneer of the Conscious Aging movement. In his book *From Aging to Saging,* Schachter-Shalomi warned that if in our "elder" years we are still searching for "the more" in sex and pleasure, we are "flowing against the current of *Thanatos.*"

I reminded Ram Dass of the story he told about the older man who could kiss a frog and turn it into his own beautiful princess, but preferred "at this age" to have a talking frog.

"Which would you choose at your age now?" I asked. "A beautiful princess or a talking frog?"

Ram Dass smiled and said, "I'm gay, so he'd be a prince."

"So would you rather have a handsome prince or a talking frog?" I asked.

He thought for a moment, then answered, "Neither."

"Sex isn't gone with me," he continued, "but it's not as interesting. It's changed its power over me. I'm not driven by it the way I was for thirty-five years. I'm very relieved to have the space and time that leaves. But I'm all for older people doing it—I delight in hearing about people doing it at ninety."

I was curious about Ram Dass's opinion on the use of psychedelic drugs in later life. When a conference participant had asked him, "Are pharmaceuticals in your life at this time?" he had said, "Yes, I love psychedelics, I honor them. They played a key role in my development. But chemicals in general are a social problem when used for escapism, all the way from Prozac to heroin."

In *The Only Dance There Is,* Ram Dass said he was able to experience "almost all of the states I have experienced with LSD" through his practice of *pranayama* (control of breathing). I asked if he still practices *pranayama*.

"I don't do it now," he said. "To be able to do it, you have to watch your diet. You can't be living and eating in Ramada Inns; it's too emotionally unstable."

Does he meditate every day?

"No, I do it most of the time. I try to make my life into a meditative practice."

When Richard Alpert met his guru, Neem Karoli Baba, in India in 1967, it "changed the course of [his] life" and transformed him into Ram Dass.

Does he think of himself as a guru?

"No. People have enticed me. It's too absurd. They offer a throne and robes. I tell them, 'My guide was an old Indian with his blanket falling off.' Besides, why would you want to be a guru? I don't want to be in the hotel business.

"There are some people from India coming over tonight, and they'll bring me candy and flowers, they'll touch my feet, have their children touch my feet. I'm their projection; I'm fodder for them, a pawn in their game. It's a way to contribute to them, to serve them. I don't take their projection of me any more seriously than if someone says 'Ram Dass, you're full of shit.' I stop, look to see if I am full of shit, and if I am, I do something about it. If I'm not, I forget about it."

I asked Ram Dass his plans for the future.

"My guru said, 'No monasteries or ashrams for you, Ram Dass. You don't stay put, you keep moving.' I'm part of a sect that believes water and yogis turn bad by staying in one place. It's a lineage of service. It's karma yoga, the path of service to liberation.

"I have no students. It really wouldn't be appropriate. I'm more like an elementary school teacher. I don't give graduate course work. What I do is great karma. *Be Here Now* touched a lot of people's lives. The people I work with, their love and appreciation comes from such a sweet, deep place. It's not like a fan club; it's genuine."

Ram Dass's many fans were distressed to learn that three years after that conference, while working on his book about conscious aging at his home in San Anselmo, California, he suffered a major stroke. His vision and hearing were impaired, and he needed to use a wheelchair, but he worked hard at recovery, and finished his book—with the wry and appropriate title *Still Here*. Six years after the stroke, though still using a wheelchair, he was carrying on his work, writing, traveling, speaking—being here, still, now.

27

Rowing toward God: Anne Sexton

Interrogator: Why talk to God?
Anne: It's better than playing bridge.
—Anne Sexton, *The Death Notebooks*

t is also riskier. As a poet and as a person, Anne Sexton continually pushed herself on to greater risks; she lived and wrote way out there on the scary edge of physical and mental survival, taunting and tempting death, doing her dark dances in places of hairbreadth danger most of us run from, and then dashing back to tell us about it and exhort us, in spite of all she'd seen and done, to "Live, Live because of the sun / the dream, the excitable gift."

Little wonder that when the "interrogator" of *The Death Notebooks* asks the "Anne" voice what she could say about her last seven days, she replies, "They were tired." She had titled her latest book *The Awful Rowing toward God*. Though I wish she would have lived and written longer—into ripe old age—I marvel now that she had the energy and courage to do it as long as she did. When in the first bright week of October 1974 she finished going over galleys of her new book with her dear friend and fellow poet

Maxine Kumin and drove home to Weston, Massachusetts, and put her car in the garage and closed the doors and kept the motor running until the unmoving auto took her where she finally had to go, she was forty-five years old.

That may not be so old for the average person, but it's a long time for one who lived and worked at the precarious pitch of her personal dialogue with God and the Devil, her private struggle with terror and an unnameable interior pain, unrelieved by psychoanalysis and aggravated by alcohol. In *The Death Notebooks* she wrote, "I am not immortal. / Faust and I are the also-ran."

My own copy of the book has a personal inscription from Anne that is typical of her generosity of spirit. She wrote: "For Wake—who first believed in Sexton—and I pray will not be put off by this title—and peeks inside—for the God in both of us."

Beside her signature she drew an impromptu flower, sprouting jauntily out of the ground, and wrote above it, with a line leading from the flower to the word *HOPE*. Knowing I was squeamish, she feared the title might scare me off, and wanted to assure me the contents were not all that depressing. As an extra pacifier to my potential fears, she drew in the hopeful flower.

Of course, I was hardly the first who "believed in Sexton" as a poet, but I was probably among the number of her early fans, due to some happy accidents of time and place. In August 1960, I was invited to the Bread Loaf Writers Conference in Vermont to give a lecture and stay for a few days' visit. Two years before, I had been a Fellow at the Conference, and on my return I was introduced to the current crop of Fellows—writers of promise who were just beginning to publish their work. One of them was an attractive young woman named Anne Sexton who had a strong voice (okay, I thought it was loud) and a resounding, almost hysterical, laugh. I was still naïve enough to think that poets expressed their "sensitivity" by looking and speaking like scared rabbits. This Sexton woman came on like a candidate for the State Assembly.

"Hey!" she called to me. "Whattya think of this title— *To Bedlam—And Part Way Back*. It's my first book of poems! 'Bedlam'—you know, the loony bin kind." I said the title seemed fine, smiled nervously, and retreated.

The following winter I went to a poetry reading at the YMHA in New York to hear an editor/poet I knew read at an evening program for new poets. When the last poet turned out to be that "Bedlam woman" I had met at Bread Loaf, I expected the worst. Then she read.

Before she even opened her mouth, and looked out over the crowd, calm and in command, she was a different person than the one I'd met. Just as some people become jittery and disoriented when they face a microphone, Anne was one of those rare ones who became at ease, even at peace. She said once that, in writing poetry, "I am the master of the poem. I control it," and she seemed to have that feeling in reading her work as well as writing it.

When she finished reading her selection from *To Bedlam—And Part Way Back,* I looked around and saw people sitting stock still in their hard metal chairs, many of them with tears that they hadn't even bothered to wipe away. I was in the same condition. The next day I bought the book. I still have it. I don't have my original because I gave it away, and since then I have bought many other copies and given them away and bought more for myself. Her work has been a sustaining factor in my life, and never so much as in that season I first read it when I was living in a scroungy apartment in Greenwich Village and going to an analyst and conducting my own experiments with razor blades and booze.

But it was not just as a kind of neurotic's notebook that those poems spoke to me. It was the writer I was trying to become that they impressed and inspired. In all the comments on the "confessional" nature of her poems, it's sometimes forgotten that she is a great storyteller. Some of her poems convey in a few pages the essence of a life.

In the spring of 1966 I reviewed her new book of poems, *Live or Die,* and ended the review with my belief that she should win the Pulitzer Prize for poetry. A month later she did. There is no connection between those two occurrences, but Anne and I had fun kidding about it. I told her it was the first time I'd ever said in print that someone should get the Pulitzer, and it would also be the last. "You're right," she said. "Stop while you're ahead!"

I did not know the dark side of Anne but rather the outgoing, charming, and often hilarious person who could joke you into a happy hysteria. The only times Anne spoke morosely to me it was not about personal anguish of any kind but about snide critics or jealous colleagues (of which there were not a few) and insensitive editors. One magazine's poetry editor especially bugged her, and his put-downs of her poems, and pompous suggestions for picayune changes, drove her up the wall. When she complained to me about this editor's latest rejection of some of her poems with a condescending comment, I said, "Listen, Anne, you mustn't pay any attention to that guy. He's what they call 'The Killer of the Dream'!"

Anne brightened; her eyes grew wide and delighted, and she said "Yes, that's it! He's 'The Killer of the Dream'!"

The notion seemed to relieve her, and in fact she improved on it. She later told me she had used it in a poem in *The Death Notebooks,* in which she eloquently summed up those petty people of the world as "the killers of the dream/the busboys of the soul."

A year before she died, Anne called and asked if I would introduce her at a poetry reading she was giving at Harvard. I said it would be an honor, and I'd be delighted. For a while she questioned me about whether I really meant it or was just being polite. When I finally convinced her I would love to introduce her, her voice changed; the nervousness left, and in stern, practical tones, she told me exactly how I should do it. First, I should be brief. Next, I was to tell the story she liked about how we met and how I became a fan of hers. I was also to mention that her books would be on sale in the hallway after the reading. I agreed to all terms, unconditionally.

When we arrived at a side door of Harvard's Sanders Theatre and saw four or five students standing outside, Anne cried out, "O Lord. That's all that's come. Only four or five people for that huge hall!"

It turned out that the students were standing outside because the large hall was filled to capacity and overflowing.

We were late, and when Anne walked on stage, spontaneous applause broke out. She was no longer nervous now that she faced the packed house, and she gave me one last stage instruction. She would not be sitting in the chair provided for her when I introduced her; rather, she wanted to stand so the audience would have an opportunity to see her in full view.

"They like to see what I look like," she explained, "and once I get behind the podium they can only see part of me."

She stood behind me, tall and grand, in a long black-and-white gown. When I finished my brief remarks I hurried offstage and down to the front row to watch. The audience, mostly collegiate, was with her all the way. Some young men and women ran down and knelt in front of the stage to get a closer view, like kids at a rock concert. One entranced fellow tried to imitate her gestures, as her long, graceful hands became serpents, then swans, while she read. I have never witnessed a more successful poetry reading, never seen an audience more appreciative, a poet more deeply appreciated.

That must have made it all the more shocking when Anne read the snide little notice in the next morning's *Boston Globe* by a reporter whose nastily misconstrued account of the evening places him securely in the ranks of "the busboys of the soul."

Anne thumbtacked the "review" of her reading to the bulletin board of the English Department at Boston University, where she taught a highly regarded and extremely popular poetry seminar in the Graduate School of Writing. She scrawled in the margin of the newspaper that this should be a lesson to student poets not to pay attention to anyone, not to let teachers or editors or critics pull you down, that even "at the so-called top" you got hit with such "spitballs." She had a medallion she wore as a necklace with an inscription on the back that said, "Don't let the bastards get you."

The bastards and the busboys annoyed Anne Sexton, but they didn't "get" her. She dealt with real demons. In recording the battles with her own dragons, she illuminated the darkness of the nightmares of others; as Kurt Vonnegut appreciatively put it, she "domesticated our terror." Looking back over all her poems, I want to think of her in the peace and simplicity suggested by the last lines of "A Story for Rose" in her first book:

We bank over Boston. I am safe.
I put on my hat.
I am almost someone going home.
The story has ended.

28

A Believing Nonbeliever:
Leonard Kriegel

The young Leonard Kriegel's dreams of baseball glory—not to speak of a normal life—were steamed away at age eleven in the daily hot-water immersions that failed to restore the use of his legs, which were paralyzed by polio. The virus that struck this country in 1944 sentenced the Bronx boy to life in a wheelchair or on crutches. How does such a devastating loss affect the work and the faith of a boy—and the man he becomes?

Leonard Kriegel became a writer and teacher determined to challenge the limits of his condition. In robbing him of his ability to run or even walk, Kriegel says polio in return gave him "a writer's voice" and taught him "how to see and what to look for." Inspired by a love of books and the sound of sentences, fueled by rage at his physical loss and a fiery commitment to speak the truth about his condition, Kriegel has fashioned a powerful body of work, including his memoir, *The Long Walk Home*; a book of essays, *Flying Solo: Reimagining Manhood, Courage and Loss*; and a novel, *Quitting Time*, that tells the story of a Jewish immigrant (like his parents) who becomes a labor leader. In his later work he explores the meaning of God in his life as a "cripple"—

the word he proudly insists on as a label for his condition. In an interview with Kriegel I asked him about his views on these issues.

DW: *You write about yourself—and want others to describe you—as a "cripple." When did you first think of yourself as a cripple and begin to take on that identity?*

LK: I got polio when I was eleven, and until I was seventeen, I couldn't admit to myself that I was never going to be a major league ballplayer. I had a very vivid fantasy life. Then one day, a month short of my seventeenth birthday, I was looking out my bedroom window, watching my friends and my kid brother playing stickball, and I suddenly realized that I would never play ball again, because I was a cripple, and that's not what a cripple did. I sat up in bed and began pounding my fists on the windowsill and weeping with rage. I slammed my fists down until my knuckles were raw and bloody.

My anger that morning was cleansing. From that point on, I accepted the fact that I was a cripple—and that, as a cripple, I was as responsible for my own life as anyone else was for his. I decided I would make this condition a part of myself. You have to accept your limitations before you can consciously set about trying to overcome them. Like F. Scott Fitzgerald's young Gatsby, I made a list of all the things I wanted to accomplish and what it would take to do them. I remember being upset that I couldn't learn to fly an airplane. Back then, you had to control the rudder with your feet. Now they have instruments that enable you to control the rudder with your hands, but I would no more try to fly today than try to swim the Atlantic; the very idea terrifies me. Until I was well into my thirties, however, I had to try everything. Sure, it was a form of compensation—even over-compensation—but that didn't take away the satisfaction of having done something I wasn't supposed to be able to do. I'm not saying anyone else has to do the same, but for me it worked.

DW: And using the word "cripple" was part of that acceptance and challenge?

LK: Absolutely. I don't object to the words "handi-capped" and "disabled," but they seem softer, more abstract, than "crippled." The term that really offends me is "differently abled." When I hear somebody say that, I want to take my crutch and wrap it around his head.

Listen, you have to earn the right to call yourself crippled. You earn it by trying to stand that word's definition on its head. "Differently abled" abstracts from illness. It takes away your need to do something about illness; it takes away the idea that you can confront your condition with courage and dignity, giving meaning to your pain without wallowing in it.

DW: I once used the word "crippled" in a book review for the New York Times, *because the author whose book I was writing about used the word, but the editors told me I had to change it. Have people ever asked you to use another word for your condition?*

LK: Yes, and I've argued the point. I think "crippled" is the best word because it's the most accurate. As a writer, I think language is supposed to be strong and definitive, and should speak of what is. Even the sound of "crippled" tells you something. It has a harshness about it that speaks to the condition. The writer's job is to communicate an experience, and when you abstract from it with terms like "differently abled," there's no way you can communicate the pain of not being able to use your legs and the rage that is an inevitable concomitant of that pain.

DW: I know you're not a "believer" in any orthodox sense, yet you often seem engaged with the issue of faith in your writing.

LK: I think there should be a category called "believing nonbeliever." That's how I classify myself. I'm a person who, on the one hand, yearns for faith, and yet, on the other hand, doesn't completely feel it. I despise absolutism of any kind. I despise faith that's self-righteous, and I despise those who are equally self-righteous in their denial of faith.

DW: In one of your essays, you speak of being "fearful of the pull of faith." Why?

LK: That's an attitude I have toward many things. For instance, I wanted to be a parent, yet the idea of being responsible for another life scared the hell out of me. There are any number of things you want and don't want at the same time. People ask me, "How can you argue with a God you claim not to believe in?" I say, "The same way you argue with a God you do believe in."

In 1969, I was driving across Germany with my family, and we stopped in Munich. The hotel where we stayed was on Dachaustrasse. I asked my wife to take the kids to the park while I drove up to Dachau alone. There was a monument there, and I thought I should say *kaddish* [the Hebrew prayer for the dead], but I couldn't. The words just wouldn't come.

Then, three years ago, in Washington, D.C., I went to the

Holocaust Museum, which I'd been opposed to building, and I found the experience incredibly moving. I stayed for two and a half hours, and at the end I saw in a glass case a Raggedy Ann doll that had belonged to a girl eleven years old—exactly the age I was when I got polio. She'd been put on a train to the death camp, the exhibit said, but the train had had an accident, and she'd escaped. They'd hunted her down and shot her and left the doll there. At that point, I just broke down.

Reading that little story was like reading James Baldwin: you can read about the horror of slavery, but it doesn't quite seem real. Then you read about this guy who goes to De Witt Clinton High School and wants to be a writer, and the world is determined to make him feel like a worm, and he says, "I'm not going to feel like a worm. I'm not going to let them beat me down," and you understand. Anne Frank's diary has the same effect. I can't imagine 6 million peanuts, much less 6 million people, but I can see this one girl and understand. There's something very real about this adolescent girl who can't stand her mother and is cooped up in a cramped attic. What made the Holocaust real for me was that one little doll in a museum. And I don't even know how many members of my family were killed—only one uncle escaped, by fleeing to Russia. After I saw that rag doll and read its story, I went into the meditation room at the end of the exhibit, and I stood there and recited *kaddish*.

I claim not to believe, but when my father died I said *kaddish* every morning and night for a year. I think we all seek spiritually; I just can't say that I've found. At the same time, I can't say I haven't found. I'm always balancing the secular and the spiritual in work. I come down on the side of intense confusion. I wouldn't call myself a believer but a man yearning for belief—which is why I also wouldn't call myself a nonbeliever.

I might use the word *agnostic,* admitting to the possibility of God as well as to the possibility of accident. I would prefer it weren't accident, but I can't necessarily believe what I prefer. When I was growing up, being an atheist held a certain glamour. It was considered brave. There was something tough and defiant about it. But today, for me, being an atheist would be an embarrassment. One thing I insist on in my own writing is absolute honesty—it's the only reason to write autobiographically. When either spirituality or nonbelief becomes smug, I can't stand it. The two seem to me parallel states of officiousness. I'd rather live with doubt and hope.

29

Better Than Church Spires: Norm Eddy

The growing plague of heroin addiction in the 1950s was brought to the attention of Eisenhower-era America by the movie *The Man with the Golden Arm,* based on Nelson Algren's hard-hitting novel, and starring Frank Sinatra as a junkie poker dealer. The problem was brought to the attention of a young minister in East Harlem in a more immediate way by a seventeen-year-old Puerto Rican boy who belonged to a storefront church on 100th Street. Louis "Pee Wee" Leon told Reverend Norman Eddy that the lives of his friends and neighbors were being destroyed by the drug, and asked, "What are we going to do?"

"Like all good Americans," Norm recalled many years later with a wry smile, "we formed a committee."

The Narcotics Committee of the East Harlem Protestant Parish (EHPP) was not like most committees, though, for its members, guided by Norm Eddy, did not just meet and "study the problem." They actually did something about it.

"When Pee Wee Leon came to me for help in 1956," Norm told me, "there was not a single hospital or doctor in New York City or State to treat adult addicts."

The court could send addicts under twenty-one to

Riverside Hospital on North Brother Island for detoxification treatment, but the only option for adults hooked on heroin was to kick the habit cold turkey—on their own or in jail. They could petition the court to spend thirty days at the Riker's Island prison (where hard labor was prescribed for withdrawing from the drug) or check into the Federal Narcotic Facility in Lexington, Kentucky.

So what could be done to change all this by the minister of a storefront church, the church's secretary, the mother of an addicted young woman, and a high school kid? They enlisted a few other neighbors and soon had seventy-five to a hundred people coming to meetings to learn about the subject that, up to then, Norm said, had been "very hush hush." Doctors, sociologists, jazz musicians, cops, and social workers came to talk, exploding myths of addiction that flourished when the subject was taboo.

Talk became action as the EHPP Narcotics Committee and their allies picketed Metropolitan Hospital to open beds for addicts withdrawing from the drug, and state hospitals followed. The committee provided counseling, referrals, group therapy, and a "wild, rich" weekly Bible study Norm led in his living room, where people argued, shouted, vented, and found inspiration and support. Usually a warm, smiling man, Norm turned red with anger if a visitor got "too intellectual." I was there when he kicked out a visiting social worker when his comments got pretentious.

The people of 100th Street between First and Second Avenues, dubbed the "worst block in the city" by the *New York Times,* trusted this prematurely white-haired young white minister who lived on the same block. Rebelling against the Country Club Christianity of Eisenhower America, when bigger churches with taller spires were symbols of religious "success," Norm and his fellow ministers of the East Harlem Protestant Parish took literally Jesus' message of service to the poor. Like Dorothy Day and her followers in the Catholic Worker movement, they lived where they preached and what they preached.

Like most of this group ministry, Norm served in World War II (he drove an ambulance and saw action in the battle of El Alamein), graduated from Union Theological Seminary, and came from a middle-class community (Hartford, Connecticut). Norm's parents, like those of his colleagues in the parish, were shocked and dismayed that he and his wife (Reverend Margaret Eddy) not only lived in a drug- and crime-ridden neighborhood, but intended to raise their son and two daughters there. As it turned out, none of the children of the parish ministers got into drugs or crime, as so many of their suburban counterparts did.

I met Norm in 1957 when I went to East Harlem to write my first book, *Island in the City,* and I brought James Baldwin up to meet him and hear about his work. The writer asked the minister why he had come to live in that neighborhood, and Norm explained that it was not to "save souls" or "do good" in the way outsiders assumed, but rather to realize a dream: "I want to help create Plymouth Colony in East Harlem." Baldwin immediately said, "I understand." Norm told me later that Baldwin was "the first person who knew what I was talking about."

Norm also understood the dream of a young minister in the South named Martin Luther King Jr., the moment he heard about it. He went to Montgomery, Alabama, to meet Dr. King in 1956, sensing that he was the man to lead the nation in the civil rights struggle. Norm felt his instinct was confirmed when he learned that King had hired a former addict from 135th Street and Lenox Avenue to be his driver.

"In those days, addicts were considered 'beyond hope,'" Norm said, and the fact that King put his trust in such a man showed he believed that people could grow and change.

That belief is a cornerstone of Norm's life and work, proved by the grassroots, inner-city groups he helped coordinate with his wife and fellow minister Peg Eddy that began on East 100th Street. The EHPP Narcotics Committee changed the laws for treatment of drug addiction; the Christian Economics Group of ten young adults saw their neighbors ruined by loan sharks and established the first inner-city credit union, while the Metro North Citizens Committee launched the neighborhood's first community housing project and rebuilt the tenements on 99th Street from Second Avenue to the East River.

Norm calls these groups that began in the 1950s and 1960s "the great-grandparents" of changes that still benefit people in New York City and State, and beyond. Norm himself is a great-grandparent who still lives in the neighborhood and carries on his work at age eighty-three, devoting himself in recent years to improving East Harlem's schools. With his spirit-guided, grassroots activism, he has proved that ministers can build more valuable legacies than church spires.

30

He Takes No Prisoners: Henri Nouwen

For all of Henri Nouwen's accomplishments and influence, he was never reviewed in the *New York Times,* never went on a major book tour, never did the TV talk show circuit, and never traveled by limousine. He simply lived and preached the Christian faith in the most powerful way I've ever witnessed.

When I met Father Nouwen in 1983, he was already a spiritual hero of mine. I had recently returned to church after a quarter-century as a card-carrying atheist. I encountered Nouwen's work when my minister gave me a copy of *Reaching Out: Three Movements in the Spiritual Life* to answer some of my religious questions. I went on to read Nouwen's powerful memoir, *Prayers from the Genesee.* The opportunity to have lunch with him was as marvelous to me as the idea of having a drink with Ernest Hemingway would have been when I was a college student.

The lunch was arranged by James Carroll, a former Paulist priest turned novelist who was writing a book about the Catholic Church during the Vietnam War era. He wanted to reminisce with Nouwen about those times and verify some of his own recollections. I was an appendage, present because of the good graces of James Carroll, so I held my peace until dessert and coffee, when Carroll told Henri of my recent return to religion.

Nouwen was in a grumpy mood because of his discomfort at Harvard Divinity School, where he was in the first year of a contract. When he turned his intimidating gaze on me I mustered the nerve to blurt out one of 6 million questions I wanted to ask.

"Father Nouwen, I've read your *Prayers from the Genesee*. What bothers me is that if someone as advanced as you has doubts and difficulties with prayer, what hope is there for someone like me who's just starting out?" Nouwen looked at me sternly and said, rather sharply, "Mr. Wakefield, Christianity is not for 'getting your life together.'"

I was taken aback, abashed. Was I getting it all wrong? In a way, yes. Nouwen was telling me that Christianity was not simply another scheme for the never-ending satisfaction of the self; it went beyond an ego trip and grew into service to others, and the giving up of self, surrendering to God. Christianity offered a journey that was not just sweetness and light but thundering darkness and doubt, thorns as well as roses, nails as well as doves. What I took at the time to be a put-down from Nouwen later came to seem like a comfort to me. When, in spite of all my efforts I still hadn't "gotten my life together," I realized that it didn't necessarily mean I wasn't a Christian.

I was not surprised by Nouwen's discomfort with Harvard. When I spent a year there once on a Nieman fellowship in journalism, I was struck by how it lived up to its reputation for academic pretentiousness. Talk about "academically correct"!

Harvard seemed to harbor a special distaste for scholars whose reputation and popularity reached beyond the academy. Nouwen had a devoted following in the outside world, as Harvard Divinity School discovered when it scheduled him for a public lecture in a room that held about a hundred people. A hundred more had to be turned away. A seminarian told me later there were condescending remarks at the Divinity School the next day about Nouwen's crowd—"all those people from the suburbs."

Those interlopers included me and a dozen or so of my fellow parishioners from King's Chapel. We were thrilled to hear Nouwen in person. We were so moved by the experience that we met afterward to discuss it at our church parish house and invited others to join us. Our efforts to convey the spirit of Nouwen's words, however, seemed pedestrian and flat.

Nouwen was a speaker like none other I have heard. He had a slight lisp, but that didn't impede his delivery, which came with and through the body—not in practiced gestures of public oratory but in an all-out effort to convey his message. It was as if he were trying literally to extract it from his heart, from the very fiber of his being, and present it to his audience, to transmit to each one of them the gift of his faith. I came away feeling that his words had been not merely spoken but implanted in us by a kind of physical-spiritual transmission, one that must have cost him a great deal.

This is not the sort of thing "one does" at Harvard, at least not with the approbation of one's peers. After two years, Nouwen resigned and went to a position as comfortable for him as it would have been impossible for an academic don.

He became the resident pastor at Daybreak in Toronto, one of the "L'Arche" communities started by the French Canadian Jean Vanier.

At Daybreak, functioning adults live with and care for people who would otherwise be confined to mental institutions. Nouwen woke each morning to bathe, dress, and feed a man incapable of performing those tasks for himself. When he traveled to speaking engagements (there were always more requests than he had time to fill), he insisted that the sponsoring organization help him bring along one of the mentally impaired people from his community. He made them part of his life and work, and projected them into the consciousness of those who came to hear him.

"There is a man who lives in my community who asks me, 'What are you doing here?' every time I see him," Nouwen recounted in a homily, "and a woman there who smiles and says, 'Welcome!' whenever I see her. I could regard these people as mentally handicapped, or I could see them as angels who are bringing me important messages every day—to ask myself what I'm doing with my life on earth, and to remind me that I am welcome here."

He expressed a living, day-to-day faith, a hard faith, as difficult as it was glorious, and he forced you by the power of his belief and his commitment to consider your own life and faith or lack of it. As Mary Rourke of the *Los Angeles Times* perceptively observed, "Nouwen isn't the sort of man the world is aching to meet."

After Nouwen spoke at a conference in Berkeley sponsored by *Image: A Journal of Religion and the Arts,* I walked out of the assembly with a woman who had never heard Nouwen before. I asked her what she thought.

She stopped, considered for a moment, then said, "He takes no prisoners."

I sat next to Nouwen at a dinner at that conference on spirituality and art, and I feared he might nod off from boredom. Then a woman at the head of the table complained that she couldn't continue being a Catholic because she disagreed with the politics of the church. Suddenly coming to life, Nouwen leaned across his plate to speak to her. "All that is distraction," he said. "I don't mean to denigrate or even dispute your complaints, but those are beside the point. The only thing that really matters is your relationship with Jesus—I mean a personal relationship with the mystical Jesus."

The woman looked stunned and confused. Imagining what she might be thinking, I asked Nouwen, "How does someone have a relationship with the 'mystical Jesus'? That sounds like a pretty awesome undertaking."

"Just give me ten minutes a day," Nouwen said with passion. "No—five minutes! Just take five minutes a day, every day for two weeks, to sit quietly and ask to be with Jesus, and ask for his presence. Then come and tell me what's important!"

Pushing his plate aside so he could sit even closer to the woman, Nouwen said with electric intensity, "People complain about the church—they say the church isn't interested in their problems. I spoke to a young man with AIDS a few days ago who told me, 'The church doesn't care about me. Where is the church in my life now when I'm dying of AIDS?' And I said, 'Who do you think *I* am? Who do you think any priest is? *I am the church, and I care about you. That's why I'm here with you now.'*"

At that same dinner a publisher boasted that his firm had just signed up the Dalai Lama for a ten-book, million-dollar-plus contract, and many there were in awe. I was happy for the Dalai Lama, whom I regard with the greatest respect and appreciation, but I couldn't help thinking, "Here in this room is a writer with a message from the heritage of your own culture, whose works have inspired countless people, and whose message will last, and you don't even approach him."

Henri Nouwen was looking for a publisher. He wanted support for a book he wanted to write about a group of acrobats he had come to know while on a trip to Germany, and how their high-wire work was an analogy for the Spirit, the life of faith. I urged a number of agents and publishers to go see him in Toronto, to give him what he needed in order to take the time to write this book. No one bothered.

Nouwen wrote and published more than thirty books, taught thousands of seminary students, was a friend and mentor to countless seekers as well as believers he inspired and who will never forget him. Of all his work and all his words I most treasure a passage in *Reaching Out* that carries his message of the hope and promise of faith:

> *What if the events of our history are molding us as a sculptor molds his clay, and it is only in a careful obedience to these molding hands that we can discover our real vocation and become mature people? What if all the unexpected interruptions are in fact the invitations to give up old-fashioned and outmoded styles of living*

and are opening up new unexplored areas of experience? And finally, what if our histories do not prove to be a blind impersonal sequence of events over which we have no control, but rather reveal to us a guiding hand pointing to a personal encounter in which all our hopes and aspirations will reach their fulfillment? Then our life would indeed be different, because then fate becomes opportunity, wounds a warning and paralysis an invitation to search for deeper sources of vitality.

ABOUT THE AUTHOR

Dan Wakefield is a novelist, journalist, and screenwriter whose books on spirituality include *Returning: A Spiritual Journey; The Story of Your Life: Writing a Spiritual Autobiography; Expect a Miracle: The Miraculous Things That Happen to Ordinary People;* and *Releasing the Creative Spirit: Unleashing the Creativity in Your Life* (SkyLight Paths). He gives workshops in Spiritual Autobiography and Creativity in churches, synagogues, adult education centers, health spas, and prisons throughout the country.

Wakefield's novels include the best-sellers *Starting Over* and *Going All the Way,* both of which were produced as feature films. His memoir of *New York in the 50s* is the basis of a documentary film that was shown theatrically and on the Sundance Channel.

He is writer-in-residence at Florida International University in Miami, and can be reached via his website, DanWakefield.com.

About SKYLIGHT PATHS Publishing

SkyLight Paths Publishing is creating a place where people of different spiritual traditions come together for challenge and inspiration, a place where we can help each other understand the mystery that lies at the heart of our existence.

Through spirituality, our religious beliefs are increasingly becoming a part of our lives—rather than *apart* from our lives. While many of us may be more interested than ever in spiritual growth, we may be less firmly planted in traditional religion. Yet, we do want to deepen our relationship to the sacred, to learn from our own as well as from other faith traditions, and to practice in new ways.

SkyLight Paths sees both believers and seekers as a community that increasingly transcends traditional boundaries of religion and denomination—people wanting to learn from each other, *walking together, finding the way.*

We at SkyLight Paths take great care to produce beautiful books that present meaningful spiritual content in a form that reflects the art of making high quality books. Therefore, we want to acknowledge those who contributed to the production of this book.

PRODUCTION
Tim Holtz & Briana Otranto

EDITORIAL
Amanda Dupuis, Maura D. Shaw & Emily Wichland

COVER DESIGN
Tim Holtz

TEXT DESIGN
Dawn DeVries Sokol, Tempe, Arizona

PRINTING & BINDING
Lake Book, Melrose Park, Illinois

Other Interesting Books—Spirituality

Releasing the Creative Spirit: *Unleash the Creativity in Your Life*
by *Dan Wakefield*

**From the author of *How Do We Know When It's God?*—
a practical guide to accessing creative power in every area of your life.**

Explodes the myths associated with the creative process and shows how everyone can uncover and develop their natural ability to create. Drawing on religion, psychology, and the arts, Dan Wakefield teaches us that the key to creation of any kind is clarity—of body, mind, and spirit—and he provides practical exercises that each of us can do to access that centered quality that allows creativity to shine. 7 x 10, 256 pp, Quality PB, ISBN 1-893361-36-5 **$16.95**

Creating a Spiritual Retirement
A Guide to the Unseen Possibilities in Our Lives
by *Molly Srode*

Discover how retirement can lead to new spiritual possibilities.

Invites you to examine your spiritual life and explore ways of making it more meaningful: contemplate the possibilities for spiritual growth that come with retirement from the daily workplace; discover how to look for the sacred in this life, in both ordinary and extraordinary ways; create your path to more fully develop a spiritual practice to provide support, strength, challenge, and comfort in the later years of life. 6 x 9, 208 pp, HC, ISBN 1-893361-75-6 **$19.95**

Spiritual Innovators: *Seventy-Five Extraordinary People Who Changed the World in the Past Century*
Edited by *Ira Rifkin* and *the Editors at SkyLight Paths*; Foreword by *Robert Coles*

Black Elk, H. H. the Dalai Lama, Abraham Joshua Heschel, Martin Luther King, Jr., Krishnamurti, C. S. Lewis, Aimee Semple McPherson, Thomas Merton, Elijah Muhammad, Simone Weil, and many more.

Profiles of the most important spiritual leaders of the past one hundred years. An invaluable reference of twentieth-century religion and an inspiring resource for spiritual challenge today. Authoritative list of seventy-five includes mystics and martyrs, intellectuals and charismatics from the East and West. For each, includes a brief biography, inspiring quotes, and resources for more in-depth study.
6 x 9, 304 pp, b/w photographs, Quality PB, ISBN 1-893361-50-0 **$16.95**;
HC, ISBN 1-893361-43-8 **$24.95**

Or phone, fax, mail or e-mail to: SKYLIGHT PATHS Publishing
Sunset Farm Offices, Route 4 • P.O. Box 237 • Woodstock, Vermont 05091
Tel: (802) 457-4000 • Fax: (802) 457-4004 • www.skylightpaths.com
Credit card orders: (800) 962-4544 (8:30AM–5:30PM ET Monday–Friday)
Generous discounts on quantity orders. SATISFACTION GUARANTEED. Prices subject to change.

Spiritual Practice

Women Pray
Voices through the Ages, from Many Faiths, Cultures, and Traditions
Edited and with introductions by *Monica Furlong*

Many ways—new and old—to communicate with the Divine.

This beautiful gift book celebrates the rich variety of ways women around the world have called out to the Divine—with words of joy, praise, gratitude, wonder, petition, longing, and even anger—from the ancient world up to our own time. Prayers from women of nearly every religious or spiritual background give us an eloquent expression of what it means to communicate with God. 5 x7¼, 256 pp, Deluxe HC with ribbon marker, ISBN 1-893361-25-X **$19.95**

Praying with Our Hands: *Twenty-One Practices of Embodied Prayer from the World's Spiritual Traditions*
by *Jon M. Sweeney*; Photographs by *Jennifer J. Wilson*;
Foreword by *Mother Tessa Bielecki*; Afterword by *Taitetsu Unno, Ph.D.*

A spiritual guidebook for bringing prayer into our bodies.

This inspiring book of reflections and accompanying photographs shows us twenty-one simple ways of using our hands to speak to God, to enrich our devotion and ritual. All express the various approaches of the world's religious traditions to bringing the body into worship. Spiritual traditions represented include Anglican, Sufi, Zen, Roman Catholic, Yoga, Shaker, Hindu, Jewish, Pentecostal, Eastern Orthodox, and many others.
8 x 8, 96 pp, 22 duotone photographs, Quality PB, ISBN 1-893361-16-0 **$16.95**

The Sacred Art of Listening
Forty Reflections for Cultivating a Spiritual Practice
by *Kay Lindahl*; Illustrations by *Amy Schnapper*

More than ever before, we need to embrace the skills and practice of listening. You will learn to: Speak clearly from your heart • Communicate with courage and compassion • Heighten your awareness for deep listening • Enhance your ability to listen to people with different belief systems. 8 x 8, 160 pp, Illus., Quality PB, ISBN 1-893361-44-6 **$16.95**

Labyrinths from the Outside In
Walking to Spiritual Insight—a Beginner's Guide
by *Donna Schaper* and *Carole Ann Camp*

The user-friendly, interfaith guide to making and using labyrinths— for meditation, prayer, and celebration.

Labyrinth walking is a spiritual exercise *anyone* can do. This accessible guide unlocks the mysteries of the labyrinth for all of us, providing ideas for using the labyrinth walk for prayer, meditation, and celebrations to mark the most important moments in life. Includes instructions for making a labyrinth of your own and finding one in your area.
6 x 9, 208 pp, b/w illus. and photographs, Quality PB, ISBN 1-893361-18-7 **$16.95**

Religious Etiquette/Reference

How to Be a Perfect Stranger, 3rd Edition
The Essential Religious Etiquette Handbook
Edited by *Stuart M. Matlins* and *Arthur J. Magida*

The indispensable guidebook to help the well-meaning guest when visiting other people's religious ceremonies.

A straightforward guide to the rituals and celebrations of the major religions and denominations in the United States and Canada from the perspective of an interested guest of any other faith, based on information obtained from authorities of each religion. Belongs in every living room, library, and office.

COVERS:

African American Methodist Churches • Assemblies of God • Baha'i • Baptist • Buddhist • Christian Church (Disciples of Christ) • Christian Science (Church of Christ, Scientist) • Churches of Christ • Episcopalian and Anglican • Hindu • Islam • Jehovah's Witnesses • Jewish • Lutheran • Mennonite/Amish • Methodist • Mormon (Church of Jesus Christ of Latter-day Saints) • Native American/First Nations • Orthodox Churches • Pentecostal Church of God • Presbyterian • Quaker (Religious Society of Friends) • Reformed Church in America/Canada • Roman Catholic • Seventh-day Adventist • Sikh • Unitarian Universalist • United Church of Canada • United Church of Christ

6 x 9, 432 pp, Quality PB, ISBN 1-893361-67-5 **$19.95**

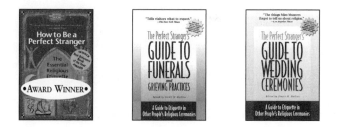

Also available:

The Perfect Stranger's Guide to Funerals and Grieving Practices
A Guide to Etiquette in Other People's Religious Ceremonies
Edited by *Stuart M. Matlins*
6 x 9, 240 pp, Quality PB, ISBN 1-893361-20-9 **$16.95**

The Perfect Stranger's Guide to Wedding Ceremonies
A Guide to Etiquette in Other People's Religious Ceremonies
Edited by *Stuart M. Matlins*
6 x 9, 208 pp, Quality PB, ISBN 1-893361-19-5 **$16.95**

SkyLight Illuminations Series
Andrew Harvey, series editor

Offers today's spiritual seeker an enjoyable entry into the great classic texts of the world's spiritual traditions. Each classic is presented in an accessible translation, with facing pages of guided commentary from experts, giving you the keys you need to understand the history, context, and meaning of the text. This series enables readers of all backgrounds to experience and understand classic spiritual texts directly, and to make them a part of their lives. Andrew Harvey writes the foreword to each volume, an insightful, personal introduction to each classic.

Bhagavad Gita: *Annotated & Explained*
Translation by *Shri Purohit Swami*; Annotation by *Kendra Crossen Burroughs*
"The very best Gita for first-time readers." —Ken Wilber
Millions of people turn daily to India's most beloved holy book, whose universal appeal has made it popular with non-Hindus and Hindus alike. This edition introduces you to the characters; explains references and philosophical terms; shares the interpretations of famous spiritual leaders and scholars; and more. 5½ x 8½, 192 pp, Quality PB, ISBN 1-893361-28-4 **$16.95**

The Way of a Pilgrim: *Annotated & Explained*
Translation and annotation by *Gleb Pokrovsky*
The classic of Russian spirituality—now with facing-page commentary that illuminates and explains the text for you.
This delightful account is the story of one man who sets out to learn the prayer of the heart—also known as the "Jesus prayer"—and how the practice transforms his existence. This edition guides you through an abridged version of the text with facing-page annotations explaining the names, terms and references. 5½ x 8½, 160 pp, Quality PB, ISBN 1-893361-31-4 **$14.95**

The Gospel of Thomas: *Annotated & Explained*
Translation and annotation by *Stevan Davies*
The recently discovered mystical sayings of Jesus—now with facing-page commentary that illuminates and explains the text for you.
Discovered in 1945, this collection of aphoristic sayings sheds new light on the origins of Christianity and the intriguing figure of Jesus, portraying the Kingdom of God as a present fact about the world, rather than a future promise or future threat. This edition guides you through the text with annotations that focus on the meaning of the sayings, ideal for readers with no previous background in Christian history or thought.
5½ x 8½, 192 pp, Quality PB, ISBN 1-893361-45-4 **$16.95**

SkyLight Illuminations Series
Andrew Harvey, series editor

Zohar: *Annotated & Explained*
Translation and annotation by *Daniel C. Matt*

The cornerstone text of Kabbalah.

The best-selling author of *The Essential Kabbalah* brings together in one place the most important teachings of the *Zohar*, the canonical text of Jewish mystical tradition. Guides you step by step through the midrash, mystical fantasy and Hebrew scripture that make up the *Zohar*, explaining the inner meanings in facing-page commentary. Ideal for readers without any prior knowledge of Jewish mysticism.

5½ x 8½, 176 pp, Quality PB, ISBN 1-893361-51-9 **$15.95**

Selections from the Gospel of Sri Ramakrishna
Annotated & Explained
Translation by *Swami Nikhilananda*; Annotation by *Kendra Crossen Burroughs*

The words of India's greatest example of God-consciousness and mystical ecstasy in recent history.

Introduces the fascinating world of the Indian mystic and the universal appeal of his message that has inspired millions of devotees for more than a century. Selections from the original text and insightful yet unobtrusive commentary highlight the most important and inspirational teachings. Ideal for readers without any prior knowledge of Hinduism.

5½ x 8½, 240 pp, b/w photographs, Quality PB, ISBN 1-893361-46-2 **$16.95**

 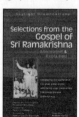  

Dhammapada: *Annotated & Explained*
Translation by *Max Müller* and revised by *Jack Maguire*; Annotation by *Jack Maguire*

The classic of Buddhist spiritual practice.

The Dhammapada—words spoken by the Buddha himself over 2,500 years ago—is notoriously difficult to understand for the first-time reader. Now you can experience it with understanding even if you have no previous knowledge of Buddhism. Enlightening facing-page commentary explains all the names, terms, and references, giving you deeper insight into the text.

5½ x 8½, 160 pp, Quality PB, ISBN 1-893361-42-X **$14.95**

Hasidic Tales: *Annotated & Explained*
Translation and annotation by *Rabbi Rami Shapiro*

The legendary tales of the impassioned Hasidic rabbis.

The allegorical quality of Hasidic tales can be perplexing. Here, they are presented as stories rather than parables, making them accessible and meaningful. Each demonstrates the spiritual power of unabashed joy, offers lessons for leading a holy life, and reminds us that the Divine can be found in the everyday. Annotations explain theological concepts, introduce major characters, and clarify references unfamiliar to most readers.

5½ x 8½, 240 pp, Quality PB, ISBN 1-893361-86-1 **$16.95**

Children's Spirituality

Ten Amazing People
And How They Changed the World
For ages 7 & up

by *Maura D. Shaw*; Foreword by *Dr. Robert Coles*
Full-color illus. by *Stephen Marchesi*

Black Elk • Dorothy Day • Malcolm X • Mahatma Gandhi •
Martin Luther King, Jr. • Mother Teresa • Janusz Korczak •
Desmond Tutu • Thich Nhat Hanh • Albert Schweitzer

This vivid, inspirational, and authoritative book will open new possibilities for children by telling the stories of how ten of the past century's greatest leaders changed the world in important ways.

8½, x 11, 48 pp, HC, Full-color illus., ISBN 1-893361-47-0 **$17.95**

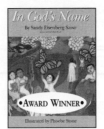

God's Paintbrush
For ages 4 & up

by *Sandy Eisenberg Sasso*; Full-color illus. by *Annette Compton*

Invites children of all faiths and backgrounds to encounter God openly in their own lives. Wonderfully interactive; provides questions adult and child can explore together at the end of each episode. "An excellent way to honor the imaginative breadth and depth of the spiritual life of the young." —Dr. Robert Coles, Harvard University

11 x 8½, 32 pp, HC, Full-color illus., ISBN 1-879045-22-2 **$16.95**

Also available:

A Teacher's Guide 8½ x 11, 32 pp, PB, ISBN 1-879045-57-5 **$8.95**

God's Paintbrush Celebration Kit 9½ x 12, HC, Includes 5 sessions/40 full-color Activity Sheets and Teacher Folder with complete instructions, ISBN 1-58023-050-4 **$21.95**

In God's Name
For ages 4 & up

by *Sandy Eisenberg Sasso*; Full-color illus. by *Phoebe Stone*

Like an ancient myth in its poetic text and vibrant illustrations, this award-winning modern fable about the search for God's name celebrates the diversity and, at the same time, the unity of all the people of the world. "What a lovely, healing book!" —Madeleine L'Engle

9 x 12, 32 pp, HC, Full-color illus., ISBN 1-879045-26-5 **$16.95**

Also available in Spanish:

El nombre de Dios 9 x 12, 32 pp, HC, Full-color illus., ISBN 1-893361-63-2 **$16.95**

Where Does God Live?
For ages 3–6

by *August Gold* and *Matthew J. Perlman*

Using simple, everyday examples that children can relate to, this colorful book helps young readers develop a personal understanding of God.

10 x 8½, 32 pp, Quality PB, Full-color photo illus., ISBN 1-893361-39-X **$8.95**

Spirituality

Journeys of Simplicity
Traveling Light with Thomas Merton, Bashō, Edward Abbey, Annie Dillard & Others
by *Philip Harnden*

There is a more graceful way of traveling through life.

Offers vignettes of forty "travelers" and the few ordinary things they carried with them—from place to place, from day to day, from birth to death. What Thoreau took to Walden Pond. What Thomas Merton packed for his final trip to Asia. What Annie Dillard keeps in her writing tent. What an impoverished cook served M. F. K. Fisher for dinner. Much more.

"'How much should I carry with me?' is the quintessential question for any journey, especially the journey of life. Herein you'll find sage, sly, wonderfully subversive advice."
—Bill McKibben, author of *The End of Nature* and *Enough*
5 x 7¼, 128 pp, HC, ISBN 1-893361-76-4 **$16.95**

The Alphabet of Paradise
An A–Z of Spirituality for Everyday Life
by *Howard Cooper*

"An extraordinary book." —Karen Armstrong

One of the most eloquent new voices in spirituality, Howard Cooper takes us on a journey of discovery—into ourselves and into the past—to find the signposts that can help us live more meaningful lives. In twenty-six engaging chapters—from A to Z—Cooper spiritually illuminates the subjects of daily life, using an ancient Jewish mystical method of interpretation that reveals both the literal and more allusive meanings of each. Topics include: Awe, Bodies, Creativity, Dreams, Emotions, Sports, and more.
5 x 7¾, 224 pp, Quality PB, ISBN 1-893361-80-2 **$16.95**

Winter: *A Spiritual Biography of the Season*
Edited by *Gary Schmidt* and *Susan M. Felch*; Illustrations by *Barry Moser*

Explore how the dormancy of winter can be a time of spiritual preparation and transformation.

In thirty stirring pieces, *Winter* delves into the varied feelings that winter conjures in us, calling up both the barrenness and the beauty of the natural world in wintertime. Includes selections by Will Campbell, Rachel Carson, Annie Dillard, Donald Hall, Ron Hansen, Jane Kenyon, Jamaica Kincaid, Barry Lopez, Kathleen Norris, John Updike, E. B. White, and many others.

"This outstanding anthology features top-flight nature and spirituality writers on the fierce, inexorable season of winter.... Remarkably lively and warm, despite the icy subject."
—★*Publishers Weekly* Starred Review
6 x 9, 288 pp, 6 b/w illus., Deluxe PB w/flaps, ISBN 1-893361-92-6 **$18.95**;
HC, ISBN 1-893361-53-5 **$21.95**

Spiritual Biography

The Life of Evelyn Underhill
An Intimate Portrait of the Groundbreaking Author of Mysticism
by *Margaret Cropper;* Foreword by *Dana Greene*

Evelyn Underhill was a passionate writer and teacher who wrote elegantly on mysticism, worship, and devotional life. This is the story of how she made her way toward spiritual maturity, from her early days of agnosticism to the years when her influence was felt throughout the world. 6 x 9, 288 pp, 5 b/w photos, Quality PB, ISBN 1-893361-70-5 **$18.95**

Zen Effects: *The Life of Alan Watts*
by *Monica Furlong*

The first and only full-length biography of one of the most charismatic spiritual leaders of the twentieth century—now back in print!

Through his widely popular books and lectures, Alan Watts (1915–1973) did more to introduce Eastern philosophy and religion to Western minds than any figure before or since. Here is the only biography of this charismatic figure, who served as Zen teacher, Anglican priest, lecturer, academic, entertainer, a leader of the San Francisco renaissance, and author of more than 30 books, including *The Way of Zen, Psychotherapy East and West* and *The Spirit of Zen.* 6 x 9, 264 pp, Quality PB, ISBN 1-893361-32-2 **$16.95**

Simone Weil: *A Modern Pilgrimage*
by *Robert Coles*

The extraordinary life of the spiritual philosopher who's been called both saint and madwoman.

The French writer and philosopher Simone Weil (1906–1943) devoted her life to a search for God—while avoiding membership in organized religion. Robert Coles' intriguing study of Weil details her short, eventful life, and is an insightful portrait of the beloved and controversial thinker whose life and writings influenced many (from T. S. Eliot to Adrienne Rich to Albert Camus), and continue to inspire seekers everywhere. 6 x 9, 208 pp, Quality PB, ISBN 1-893361-34-9 **$16.95**

Mahatma Gandhi: *His Life and Ideas*
by *Charles F. Andrews;* Foreword by *Dr. Arun Gandhi*

An intimate biography of one of the greatest social and religious reformers of the modern world.

Examines from a contemporary Christian activist's point of view the religious ideas and political dynamics that influenced the birth of the peaceful resistance movement, the primary tool that Gandhi and the people of his homeland would use to gain India its freedom from British rule. An ideal introduction to the life and life's work of this great spiritual leader. 6 x 9, 336 pp, 5 b/w photos, Quality PB, ISBN 1-893361-89-6 **$18.95**

Spiritual Perspectives

Explores how spiritual beliefs can inform our opinions and transform our actions in areas of social justice and societal change. Tackling the most important—and most divisive—issues of our day, this series provides easy-to-understand introductions to contemporary issues. Readers aren't told what to think; rather, they're given information—*spiritual* perspectives—in order to reach their own conclusions.

Spiritual Perspectives on America's Role as Superpower
by *the Editors at SkyLight Paths*

Are we the world's good neighbor or a global bully?

Explores broader issues surrounding the use of American power around the world, including in Iraq and the Middle East. From a spiritual perspective, what are America's responsibilities as the only remaining superpower? Contributors:

Dr. Beatrice Bruteau • Rev. Dr. Joan Brown Campbell • Tony Campolo • Rev. Forrest Church • Lama Surya Das • Matthew Fox • Kabir Helminski • Thich Nhat Hanh • Eboo Patel • Abbot M. Basil Pennington, ocso • Dennis Prager • Rosemary Radford Ruether • Wayne Teasdale • Rev. William McD. Tully • Rabbi Arthur Waskow • John Wilson

5½ x 8½, 256 pp, Quality PB, ISBN 1-893361-81-0 **$16.95**

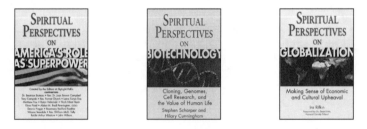

Spiritual Perspectives on Biotechnology
Cloning, Genomes, Cell Research, and the Value of Human Life
by *Stephen Scharper* and *Hilary Cunningham*

A balanced introduction to the issues of biotechnology.

From genetically modified foods through cloning of animals and life forms, explains in clear and nonjudgmental language the beliefs that motivate religious leaders, activists, theologians, academics, and others involved on all sides of biotechnology issues. Many different perspectives are included—representing all of the world's largest faith traditions and many other spiritual persuasions.

5½ x 8½, 235 pp, Quality PB, ISBN 1-893361-58-6 **$16.95**

Spiritual Perspectives on Globalization
Making Sense of Economic and Cultural Upheaval
by *Ira Rifkin*; Foreword by *Dr. David Little, Harvard Divinity School*

What is globalization? What are spiritually-minded people saying and doing about it?

This lucid introduction surveys the religious landscape, explaining in clear and nonjudgmental language the beliefs that motivate spiritual leaders, activists, theologians, academics, and others involved on all sides of the issue.

5½ x 8½, 224 pp, Quality PB, ISBN 1-893361-57-8 **$16.95**

Other Interesting Books—Spirituality

Lighting the Lamp of Wisdom: *A Week Inside a Yoga Ashram*
by *John Ittner;* Foreword by *Dr. David Frawley*

This insider's guide to Hindu spiritual life takes you into a typical week of retreat inside a yoga ashram to demystify the experience and show you what to expect from your own visit. Includes a discussion of worship services, meditation and yoga classes, chanting and music, work practice, and more.
6 x 9, 192 pp, b/w photographs, Quality PB, ISBN 1-893361-52-7 **$15.95;**
HC, ISBN 1-893361-37-3 **$24.95**

Waking Up: *A Week Inside a Zen Monastery*
by *Jack Maguire;* Foreword by *John Daido Loori, Roshi*

An essential guide to what it's like to spend a week inside a Zen Buddhist monastery.
6 x 9, 224 pp, b/w photographs, Quality PB, ISBN 1-893361-55-1 **$16.95;**
HC, ISBN 1-893361-13-6 **$21.95**

Making a Heart for God: *A Week Inside a Catholic Monastery*
by *Dianne Aprile;* Foreword by *Brother Patrick Hart, ocso*

This essential guide to experiencing life in a Catholic monastery takes you to the Abbey of Gethsemani—the Trappist monastery in Kentucky that was home to author Thomas Merton—to explore the details. "More balanced and informative than the popular *The Cloister Walk* by Kathleen Norris." —*Choice: Current Reviews for Academic Libraries*
6 x 9, 224 pp, b/w photographs, Quality PB, ISBN 1-893361-49-7 **$16.95;**
HC, ISBN 1-893361-14-4 **$21.95**

Come and Sit: *A Week Inside Meditation Centers*
by *Marcia Z. Nelson;* Foreword by *Wayne Teasdale*

The insider's guide to meditation in a variety of different spiritual traditions. Traveling through Buddhist, Hindu, Christian, Jewish, and Sufi traditions, this essential guide takes you to different meditation centers to meet the teachers and students and learn about the practices, demystifying the meditation experience.
6 x 9, 224 pp, b/w photographs, Quality PB, ISBN 1-893361-35-7 **$16.95**

Or phone, fax, mail or e-mail to: SKYLIGHT PATHS Publishing
Sunset Farm Offices, Route 4 • P.O. Box 237 • Woodstock, Vermont 05091
Tel: (802) 457-4000 • Fax: (802) 457-4004 • www.skylightpaths.com
Credit card orders: (800) 962-4544 (8:30AM–5:30PM ET Monday–Friday)
Generous discounts on quantity orders. SATISFACTION GUARANTEED. Prices subject to change.